Morocco

Pierre Loti was a member of a diplomatic mission to the Sultan of Morocco at Fez, and in this book he gives us an extraordinarily fascinating account of the journey. The departure of the caravan from Tangier, the encampments, the nightly arrival of the Mouna, the crossing of the Oued-M'Cazen in flood, the fantasies and 'powder-play' of the Arab horsemen, and the magnificent state entry into Fez, are described in a succession of vivid vignettes.

Pierre Loti, perhaps the world's most prolific, romantic and exotic travel writer and novelist, was born as Julien Marie Viaud in Rochefort in Western France in 1850. A childhood fascination with exotic lands across the seas led him to embark on a naval career that enabled him to seek love and adventure in many latitudes. He drew on these real life experiences when writing the romantic novels and travel books that made him one of the most popular authors of his day. Although his prolific output brought him both fame and fortune he remained a romantic escapist and never gave up his beloved naval career. He retired from the French navy in 1910 and died in 1923.

The Pierre Loti Library

Morocco

Pierre Loti

Routledge
Taylor & Francis Group

LONDON AND NEW YORK

First published in 2002 by
Kegan Paul International

This edition first published in 2011 by
Routledge
2 Park Square, Milton Park, Abingdon, Oxon, OX14 4RN

Simultaneously published in the USA and Canada
by Routledge
711 Third Avenue, New York, NY 10017

Routledge is an imprint of the Taylor & Francis Group, an informa business

British Library Cataloguing in Publication Data
A catalogue record for this book is available from the British Library

ISBN 10: 0-7103-0816-7 (hbk)
ISBN 13: 978-0-7103-0816-0 (hbk)

Publisher's Note
The publisher has gone to great lengths to ensure the quality of this reprint
but points out that some imperfections in the original copies may be
apparent. The publisher has made every effort to contact original copyright
holders and would welcome correspondence from those they have been
unable to trace.

MOROCCO

CHAPTER I

26th March 1889.

FROM the southern coast of Spain, from Algeciras, from Gibraltar, one may descry in the distance, on the farther shore, Tangier the White.

It is quite near our Europe, this first of Moroccan towns, posted like a sentinel on the most northern point of Africa; one may reach it by steamboat in three or four hours, and every winter it becomes the resort of a great number of tourists. It is very commonplace to-day, and the Sultan of Morocco, for his part, has half abandoned it to its foreign visitors, averting his eyes from it as from a town unfaithful.

Viewed from the sea, it looks almost smiling, with its neighbouring villas, built in the European manner in gardens; though still perhaps a little strange, and much more Mussulman in aspect than our towns of Algeria, with its walls of snowy whiteness, its high embattled *kasbah*, and its minarets decorated with old faience.

.   .   .   .

It is curious, too, how the impression on arrival

A   I

is more penetrating here than in any other of
the African ports of the Mediterranean. Despite
the tourists who disembark with me, despite the
stray French signs which here and there are
displayed before the hotels and bazaars, I
experience, as I land to-day on this quay of
Tangier in the bright noon sunshine, a sense of
translation into anterior times. How far away
all at once seem the Spain in which I was this
morning, the railway, the swift, comfortable
steamboat, the epoch in which I thought I lived !
Here, it is as if a white shroud impended over
everything, shutting out the sounds that exist
elsewhere, stilling all the modern activities of
life : the old shroud of Islam, which in a few days
no doubt, when we shall have advanced farther
into this sombre land, will envelop us more
closely, but which even now, here on the threshold, casts a spell upon us, freshly come, as we
are, from Europe.

Two attendants in the service of our Minister,
Selem and Kaddour, like Biblical figures in their
long, flowing, woollen robes, are waiting at the
landing stage to lead us to the French legation.

They precede us gravely, clearing from our
path, with sticks, the innumerable little donkeys
which take the place of barrows and carts, here
quite unknown. By a kind of narrow road we
climb to the town, between crenellated walls,

which rise in steps one above the other, mournful and white like dead snows. The people we meet, white, too, like the walls, trail their slippers through the dust with a majestic heedlessness, and merely to see them pass is to divine how little they are holden of the business of our century.

In the main street, which we have to traverse, are a number of Spanish shops, a number, too, of French and English placards, and with the white-robed crowd is mingled, alas! a number of gentlemen in cork helmets and elegant tourist misses, whose cheeks bear witness to the burning of the sun. But, for all that, Tangier is still very Arab, even in the quarter of its traders.

And, farther on, as we approach the French legation, where hospitality has been offered me, begins the labyrinth of little narrow streets swathed in white chalk, which remain intact, even as in the olden times.

CHAPTER II

On the evening of this same day of arrival, at the setting of the sun, I pay my first visit to our encampment, which is being made ready outside the walls, on a somewhat lonely height overlooking Tangier.

It is quite a little nomad town, already set up, already inhabited by the Arabs of our escort. Around, our horses, our camels, our pack-mules, tethered by ropes, are cropping a short and very fragrant grass; it might be an encampment of any tribe you please, a *douar*; the whole exhales a strong odour of Bedouin, and from the tent of the camel-drivers issue mournful songs in falsetto and thin twangings of guitars.

All this, men, beasts and material, has been sent by the Sultan to our Minister. I watch for a considerable time this congeries of men and things, which presently will accompany us in our plunge into this unknown country with which we shall have to live and share our days.

The oncoming night, the wind which rises at twilight, accentuate, as is their wont, the

4

impression of strangeness in a strange land which this Morocco made upon me from the start.

In the west the pale yellow sky, intensely cold, has an extraordinary clearness; below me, in the distance, is Tangier, looking at this hour like a scattering of cubes of stone on the slope of a mountain; its whitenesses, in the gathering dusk, assume the bluish tint of ice; beyond, stretches the deeper blue of the sea; and beyond that again, a silhouette of slate-coloured grey, is the coast of Spain, of Europe, a near neighbour with which this country, it would seem, has as little as possible to do. And this point of the world which is my world, which I left no more than a few hours ago, seen from here, seems to me all at once to have become astonishingly remote.

I return to Tangier by way of the market-place, which lies a little above the town, outside the old crenellated walls and the old ogival gates. It is nearly dark. On the ground, covering a space some hundred yards square, is a layer of brown things which grumble feebly: kneeling camels, on the point of sleeping, pell-mell with Bedouins and bales of merchandise; caravans that have set out perhaps from the confines of the desert, by routes dangerous and unmapped, to reach their journey's end here at the end of old Africa; here, in the face of the

foreland of Europe, at the threshold of our
modern civilisation.   Sounds of raucous human
voices and gruntings of beasts rise from the
confused masses which cover the ground.
Before a little fire, which burns yellow, in the
midst of a squatting circle of men, a negro
sorcerer sings softly and beats his drum.   The
night air, freshening more and more, toys
with reddish-yellow exhalations.   In its limpid
depths the sky is cove ed with stars.   And, at
this moment, an Arab bagpipe begins to wail,
dominating all other sounds with its harsh,
squeaking note.   I had forgotten this sound ;
years not a few have passed since last it
harrowed my ears.   It sets me shuddering and
leaves me with a very vivid, very thrilling
impression of Africa ; one of those impressions
of the days of arrival which are not to be renewed in the succeeding days, when the faculty
of comparison has been blunted by contact with
new things.

The bagpipe continues, with a kind of swelling
exaltation, its monotonous, heart-rending air.
I stop and listen to it.   It seems to me that the
song it sings is the hymn of ancient days, the
hymn of dead pasts.   And I feel for a moment
a strange pleasure in thinking that I am yet
only on the threshold, only at the entrance,
profaned by all the world, of this empire of Al

Moghreb into which I am soon to penetrate, that Fez, which is the goal of our journey, is far away, under the burning sun, in the heart of this closed, unchanging country, where life remains the same to-day as it was a thousand years ago.

CHAPTER III

EIGHT days of waiting, of preparations, of delays.

During this week passed at Tangier we have made numerous journeys to and fro, to examine tents, to choose and try horses and mules. And many times we have climbed the height beyond, where our camp has been gradually augmented by the addition of a considerable number of men and things—in the face always of the distant coast of Europe.

The departure is fixed at last for to-morrow morning.

Since yesterday, the approaches to the French legation have resembled a place of emigration or of pillage. The little streets, tortuous and white, of the immediate neighbourhood are encumbered with enormous bales, with hundreds of packing-cases; all covered with Moroccan cloth striped in many colours and tied with ropes of reed-grass.

CHAPTER IV

To guard our innumerable packages, our men have slept in the street, buried each in his burnous, head hidden in hood, looking like so many heaps of grey wool.

At break of day this dormant world emerges from its crouching torpor, awakens and begins to move. First, a few tentative cries, the unsteady steps of men still half-asleep ; then, almost in a moment, shouting, wrangling. The Arab language, indeed, with its harshness and panting aspirations, gives always the impression, in the mouth of men of the people, that it is the vehicle of a torrent of abuse.

And this general uproar, which increases as the minutes pass, drowns the customary sounds of the morning: the crowing of cocks, the neighing of horses, the grunting of camels in the nearest caravanserai.

Before sunrise the din has become a thing infernal : shrill cries, such as monkeys utter ; a savage hurly-burly that might well strike terror. As I lie half-awake I could imagine, if I were not used to these uproars of Africa,

9

that a fight, and one of a most barbarous kind,
was proceeding under my window ; that throats
were being cut, that destruction was afoot. But
I tell myself, simply : " Our beasts are arriving
and the muleteers are beginning to load them."

It is an awkward business, truly, to load some
five score obstinate mules and stupid camels, in
little streets that are barely two yards across.
Some of the animals, no longer finding room
to turn, neigh in distress ; some of the loads,
larger than the rest, foul the walls in passing ;
there are obstructions, collisions, kickings.

At about eight o'clock the tumult is at its
height. From the terrace of the legation, as far
as one can see in the neighbourhood, the streets
are thronged with a confused mass of men and
beasts, bellowing with all their might. Besides
the pack-mules, there are the mules of the Arabs
of our escort, harnessed in a thousand colours,
with high Arab saddles on their backs, and
housings of red, blue and yellow cloth, which
serve them as robes. Brown-visaged, white-
cloaked cavaliers are already astride them, their
long, slender guns s'ung across their shoulders.
And the whole of this caravan, which is to precede us under the conduct and responsibility of
a kaid sent by the Sultan, gets under way little
by little, laboriously, individually ; by dint of
cries and blows it all winds towards the gate of

the town, leaving at last the little streets around us empty.

Then comes the turn of the beggars—and they are many at Tangier. The fools, the idiots, the cripples, the eyeless folk with bloody sockets in place of pupils, besiege the legation to bid us good-bye. And, following custom, the Minister, appearing on the threshold, scatters some handfuls of silver coins, that he may merit for us the prayers that will bring good fortune to our caravan.

. . . .

The time of our own departure is fixed for one o'clock in the afternoon. The point of rendezvous is the market-place, there where on the evening of my arrival I had a first and unforgettable audition of the Arab bagpipe.

This vast esplanade of earth and stones lies above the town and is for ever encumbered with a compact layer of kneeling camels, for ever thronged by a cloaked and hooded crowd, which itself partakes of the dun colour of earth. Eve ything that arrives from the interior and everything that leaves to return thither is grouped and huddled in this market-place. And here, from moɪning till evening, resound the drums and pipe the flutes of the sorcerers, the casters of lots, the fire-eaters and snake-charmers.

To-day the formation of our caravan brings to the place an increase of movement and tumult. Soon after midday, in the bright sunshine, the first of our cavaliers arrive, our escort of honour, our kaids and the standard bearer of the Sultan, who, throughout the journey, will march at our head.

To-day is a market day : hundreds of camels, bald and hideous, are on their knees in the dust, stretching from right or left, with the undulations of a caterpillar, their long hairless necks; and the crowd of peasants and of poor, in grey burnouses, in *sayons* of brown wool, moves confusedly among these masses of recumbent beasts. It is an immense medley in one same dull and neutral shade, which makes all the more resplendent, in the glorious light of the distance, the town all white, surmounted by green minarets, and the Mediterranean all blue. And, against the monotonous background of this crowd, stands out more vividly, too, the Oriental colouring of the cavaliers of our suite, the caftans pink, the caftans orange, the caftans yellow, the saddles of red cloth, the saddles of velvet.

Our mission consists of fifteen persons, of whom seven of us are officers; our uniforms, also, contribute to this picture of departure a note of diversity, of colour, of gold. Five blue-cloaked African guards accompany us; and, in addition, the whole of the European colony has come on horseback to swell our train : foreign ministers, attachés of the embassy, artists, all kinds of pleasant people.

And here, too, is the Pasha of Tangier, come to conduct us out of his territory : an old man with the head of a prophet, white bearded, clothed all in white, on a red-saddled white mule led by four servants. The whole cavalcade, in its motley confusion, has an air of festive pageantry, of joyous carnival.

Let us return for a last time to bid good-bye to Tangier the White, the terraces of which slope in the distance towards the sea below our feet ; to bid good-bye above all to those blue mountains, outlined still on the farther shore of the strait, which are Andalusia, the nearest point of Europe, soon now to disappear.

It is one o'clock, the hour fixed for departure. The red silk standard of the Sultan, which is to lead us as far as Fez, is unfurled before us, topped by its copper sconce. To sound the signal to saddle we have the tabours and flutes of the sorcerers of the market-place, and our column begins to move, in much disorder, but very gaily.

On the sandy road in the outskirts of the town our horses, sharing the general gaiety, adopt the prancing movement which marks the beginning of a ride. We pass between villas European in style, before hotels where a number of fair tourist ladies are on the balconies and verandahs, grouped under umbrellas, to watch us file past. And, in all truth, we might imagine that we were simply in Algeria, at some military march, at some holiday procession; though, to be sure, the ill state of the roads and the complete absence of vehicles give to these approaches to the town an air of strangeness and singularity.

Besides, around us, the aspect of things changes very rapidly. At the end of five or six hundred yards the kind of avenue, bordered by aloes, along which we set out is lost completely in the neglected campaign; it is effaced and no longer exists. Roads there are none in Morocco, ever, anywhere. Nothing but tracks beaten in course of time by the passage of caravans, and the right to ford the rivers that lie across your path.

To-day these tracks are in doleful condition; the soil, softened by the rains of the winter, yields everywhere beneath the hoofs of our horses, which sink deep into the black mud, into the soft turf.

One after another the friends who were accompanying us forsake our party, return in their steps, after many hand-shakings and hopes of farewell. Tangier, too, has promptly disappeared, hidden by desert hills. And soon we are left alone to follow the red standard of the Sultan, we who have to continue our way for another twelve days, alone in the midst of a vast country, silent, wild, inundated with sunshine.

CHAPTER V

THE same day, at eight o'clock in the evening. In the light of a lantern, within my tent, at a nondescript place where we have camped for the night. Very lonely all at once in the midst of a profound silence, very tranquil after the activities of the day, and reclining luxuriously on my camp bed, I take pleasure in the consciousness of the wide, dark expanses that surround me, which are without roads, without houses, without shelters and without inhabitants.

The rain whips the taut canvas which serves me for walls and roof, and I hear the wind moaning. The day, which was so fine when we set out, turned dismal with the approach of night.

Our stage on this first day has been a short one : barely twelve miles. Before nightfall we perceived in the distance our little nomad town awaiting us, gay and hospitable, all white in the midst of green solitudes. Despatched early this morning on the backs of mules, it had arrived betimes, and was already unpacked, already set up, and the flags of France and

Morocco floated above it, side by side, in all friendliness.

It is the business of the kaid who has charge of the tents to see to the striking of our camp in the morning and to its pitching at night, in places always chosen in advance, near a river or a spring, and, if circumstances allow, on dry ground covered with short grass.

.   .   .   .

My bed, which is very light, is placed comfortably on my two cases, which uplift it sufficiently from the ground, the crickets and the ants ; my saddle, in guise of pillow, raises it at the head, and I am wrapped in a Moroccan blanket, striped in green and orange, of excellent wool, which keeps me very warm, what time the cool air of the night passes over me, perfumed with a wild, wholesome scent, a scent of hay and flowers. Overhead, my roof takes naturally the form of a huge umbrella ; it is white, its ribs are trimmed with blue galloons and terminated by trefoils of red Moroccan leather. All around, like one of those hanging draperies which serve to enclose circuses and merry-go-rounds, is hung a *tarabieh*—that is to say, a kind of circular wall of white canvas, embellished with the same blue ribbons, the same red trefoils, and kept in place by pegs driven into the ground. It is the uniform model of

B

all the tents proper to headmen or chiefs used in Morocco ; there would be room in it for six beds such as mine ; but the magnificence of the Sultan has given to each of us his own particular house.

For floor we have the soft sward, flowered with a minute variety of iris, a beautiful violet carpet sweetly fragrant, from the dark weft of which three or four marigolds, pinked here and there, shine out like little golden stars.

The companions of my journey and our escorting Arabs are in way of doing as I, no doubt ; they are laying them down and preparing to sleep ; in the camp, there is no longer any human sound.

And while I am enjoying the calm, the silence, the perfumed freshness, the vivifying and pure air, my eyes chance to fall, in a review casually brought, on an article by Huysmans celebrating his joy of the sleeping-car : the black smoke ; the promiscuousness and evil odours of the narrow cribs ; above all the charms of his neighbour overhead, a gentleman of two score and ten, flabby and in expectoration apt, with trinkets on his stomach, eyeglasses on his nose, and cigar between his lips. And my content grows greater to feel that I am far away from this neighbour of Huysmans— who is, as a matter of fact, a type, drawn by

the hand of a master, of the middle-aged gentleman of to-day, a mighty traveller by express.
Nay, in my delight to think that this kind
of person does not yet circulate in Morocco, I
experience a first impulse of gratitude towards
the Sultan of Fez, that he has not encouraged
the sleeping-car in his empire, but has left
us these wild pathways, where we travel on
horseback in the sweep of the wind.

.   .   .   .

At midnight the hail rattles outside and a
mighty wind shakes the canvas of my tent.
Then I hear confusedly rough voices approaching ; a lantern makes the round of my dwelling,
disclosing, in the transparency of the stretched
fabric, the black arabesques which decorate
the exterior. They are men of the watch, come,
by direction of the kaid, to tighten, by blows
of mallet, the pegs of my tent, so that the wind
may not carry it away.

I understand that when the Sultan is on his
travels, in his great tent of state, which needs
for its transport sixty mules, if by chance a
storm arise during the night, use is not made
of mallets for fear of disturbing the slumbers of
the master and of the fair ladies of the harem.
Instead, they call up a regiment of men who
crouch in circle around the nomad palace and remain there till daybreak, holding in innumerable

fingers all the ropes of the wall. One who has lived long in proximity to his Majesty told me this to-day, as our horses trotted side by side; and this sudden wind recalls it to my mind. And I fall asleep again dreaming of that Court of Fez, where dwell, veiled and immured, so many mysterious beauties.

.   .   .   .

At about two o'clock in the morning comes another nocturnal alarm : snortings of frenzied horses, galloping hoofs hammering the ground, cries of Arabs. Our beasts, which have broken loose, are stampeding, scared by I know not what invisible thing, seized by a general panic. I utter a prayer that all this may play itself out far from me ; that it may not come and entangle itself in the ropes of my tent and over-turn it. Truly, that would be an unpleasant business in the downpour which streams un-ceasingly.

Allah be praised ! The disorderly rout takes another direction, the sounds grow distant and are swallowed up in the surrounding darkness.

Then I hear them bringing back the fugitives, and calm is restored, calm and silence and sleep.

CHAPTER VI

5th April.

At six o'clock, in broad daylight, the bugle of one of our African guards sounds the réveillé.

Quickly we must arise, quickly don belt and boot; for already our Arabs have entered my little lodging, entered to demolish it—my little lodging of white canvas soaked with the rain of the night.

In a turn of the hand it is done. The wind helping, my tent flies loose, flaps for a moment like a ship's sail, then falls flat on the wet grass; and I am left in the open air, to fix my spurs and put the last touches to my toilet.

The little flowers which have slept beneath my roof are going to recover their liberty, the welcome moisture of the showers, and solitude.

And the whole of our town is dismantled in the same fashion, is folded and fastened with a multitude of cords; then saddled on the backs of kicking mules and grumbling camels; forward, our camp is struck!

. . . .

At the outset our horses frisk and neigh and rear and prance.

We begin our second day's march amid mountains covered uniformly with evergreen-oak, heather and daffodils. Scarce ever any trees in Morocco ; but, in recompense, always these grand tranquil lines of virgin country, unbroken whether by road or house or enclosure. An uncultivated land left almost in its natural state, but to all seeming marvellously fertile. Wheatfields here and there, and fields of barley, looking like meadows of a tender green. There is no obligation here to shape them to the rectangular form usual with us ; and how restful to the eye they are compared with our French campaign, all cut up and parcelled out, after the fashion of a draught-board. I have felt before, in other parts of the world, the peculiar kind of satisfaction, of ease, that is induced by these countries where space costs nothing and belongs to nobody ; it seems, too, in these countries, that the horizons expand indefinitely, that the field of vision is immeasurably enlarged, that the outspread country is without end.

And always some fifty yards ahead of us in the tranquil green distances that unroll unceasingly, always there is outlined that same advance guard which guides us and which we

follow in its continuous flight : three horsemen
side by side ; the one in the middle, a tall old
negro of majestic carriage, in caftan of pink
cloth and burnous and turban of fine white
fabric, holding high the red silk standard with
its copper sconce; his two companions, negroes
also, turbaned like their fellow, carrying their
long thin guns, the barrels of which gleam
against the bluish uniformity of the background, of the mountains and plains.

.　　.　　.　　.　　.　　.　　.

At about ten o'clock, under a grey sky, in
campaign as ever green and wild, we perceive
in front of us in the distance a motionless line
of gentlemen on horseback, who seem to be
awaiting us. We are, in fact, about to enter
new territory, and all the men of the tribe
whose hospitality we are now to enjoy are
under arms, led by their kaid, to receive us.
According to custom when an embassy travels,
they will escort us through their country, and
the others, who have accompanied us from
Tangier, will return home.

How odd they look, these cavaliers, seen in
repose and at a distance ! On their lean little
hargers, on their high Arab saddles, they look,
clike old women enveloped in long white veils
like old black-faced dolls, old mummies. They
carry very long, slender sticks covered with

shining brass—which are the barrels of their guns—their heads are swathed in muslin and their cloaks trail like shawls over the cruppers of their horses.

We draw near, and suddenly, at a signal, at a command uttered in a hoarse voice, the line disperses, swarms like a flight of bees, gambols with a clinking of arms, with a chorus of harsh cries. The horses, goaded by spur, rear, leap, gallop like frightened gazelles, tail and mane streaming in the wind, bounding over rocks and stones. And, in the same moment, the old dolls have come to life, have become superb also, have become men, slender and agile, wild and handsome of countenance, upright in their large silvered stirrups. And all the white cloaks which enwrapped them fly loose, floating behind them with an exquisite gracefulness, disclosing under-robes of red and orange and green cloth, and saddles with coverings of pink silk, of yellow silk, of blue silk embroidered with gold. And the shapely bare arms of the horsemen, of the colour of bronze, emerge from the wide sleeves that have now dropped back to the shoulder, brandishing in the air, in the mad career, the long copper guns which seem to have become as light as reeds.

It is a first fantasia of welcome given in our honour. As soon as it is finished the kaid who had superintended it advances towards our Minister and offers his hand. We bid good-bye to our companions of yesterday and continue on our way escorted by our new hosts.

CHAPTER VII

I HAVE a recollection of having traversed, throughout the whole of the afternoon of this same day, immense interminable plateaux of sand covered with bracken—such as are the Landes of the south of France. These plains were of a greenness tender and fresh beyond words, of the sweet new green of April. An attenuated ray of sunshine enlightened them obstinately, at the single precise spot at which we were, as if the gleam were following us, while, around, the mountains bounding the horizon, overhung by dark clouds, were confused with the sky in grim and sinister obscurity. Curtains of mist tempered a curious light of the colour of silver-gilt, of very pale vermeil, and to see this African campaign so green and overcast took us by surprise.

The chafing of our passage, the hoofs of the horses breaking the stems, developed very strongly the scent of the bracken, and I was reminded of the beautiful June mornings of my native land, of the arrival at market of the hampers of cherries. (In Saintonge cherries are always packed in this kind of foliage; and thus the two scents are inseparable in my remembrance.)

And every five minutes on either side of our column, in the direction opposite to our march, groups of Arab horsemen passed like the wind. On the carpet of plants, on the sand, we scarcely heard the galloping of their horses; all the noise they made in cleaving the air was a slight clinking of metal and a flapping of streaming burnouses; it seemed rather that we heard the sound of wind in the sails of a ship, or of a great flight of birds. They scarcely gave us time either to avoid being brushed by them as they swept by. And at the moment they passed us they uttered a raucous cry, then fired their long guns, covering us with smoke.

Continuously, on right or left, this rapid vision was renewed, a kind of nightmare of war, which fled extraordinarily quickly.

Only towards evening did these fantasias cease. Around us, the green colouring became more and more beautiful, the country almost wooded; there were clusters of olive-trees, and the dwarf palms were so old, so tall, that they resembled veritable trees. Hamlets appeared, here and there, on the hills; walls of beaten earth and roofs of grey thatch; the whole surrounded, guarded and half-hidden by hedges of enormous cacti almost blue in colour. And at our approach, women in rags of grey wool came out from these formidable enclosures bristling with thorns, and cried, "You! You! You!" to do us honour, in shrill, penetrating voices like those of swifts when, on summer evenings, they circle in the sky.

Later on this inhabited region disappeared, and after we had crossed two or three fords we perceived in a meadow, in a green landscape, our camp ready awaiting us. Our horses neighed with pleasure at sight of it.

.   .   .   .

Always the same, our little town, always arranged in the self-same fashion, as if it had been transported in a single piece, on wheels. And no sooner do we arrive than each of us, without loitering, betakes himself straight to his own proper dwelling, which, in relation to the others, has not changed its place ; he finds there his bed and his belongings, and, on the ground, over a first carpet of grass and flowers, his Moroccan carpet spread. We travel with all the comforts of nomads, having nothing to trouble about, nothing to do but enjoy the free air, the sense of change, of space.

Our fifteen tents form a complete circle, enclosing a kind of paddock, in which our horses graze. They are all alike, the central pole crowned by a large sconce of copper, and the

walls ornamented, on the outside, with rows
of arabesques of blue-black, which stand out
sharply against the whiteness of the whole.
(These arabesques, made of pieces of fabric
cut out and sewn on the canvas, are all of the
same design, a design extremely ancient, con-
secrated by the traditions of a thousand years :
a kind of indented crenelles repeated in rows
—the same as the Arabs carve in stone on the
summits of their religious walls, the same as
they embroider on the hem of their silken
tapestries, the same as border their mosaics of
faience, the same as are to be seen on the walls
of the Alcázar and of the Alhambra.)

And around our tents, forming a second
protecting circle, are the tents of our camel-
drivers, our muleteers, our guards; smaller and
more pointed than ours, of a uniform greyish
colour, and arranged with less regard to order,
they constitute a quarter entirely Bedouin
in character, encumbered with our beasts of
burden ; and strange music issues from them
throughout the watches of the night.

. . . .

The appearance of the *mouna* is always the
most important event of the close of a day's
march. It comes usually in the twilight, in
long procession, to be deposited finally on the
ground before the tent of our Minister. I ask

pardon for this Arab word, but our language does not possess its equivalent : *mouna* is the tithe, the ransom, which our quality of embassy gives us the right to levy upon the tribes through whose territories we pass. Without this *mouna*, commanded long in advance and brought sometimes from a great distance, we should risk dying of hunger in this country without inns, without markets, with scarce a village, almost a desert.

. . . .

The *mouna*, this evening, is of a royal abundance. In the last light of the day we see advancing into the middle of our camp a procession of grave men, clothed in white ; a handsome kaid of noble carriage marches at their head, slowly. On perceiving them, our Minister retired to his tent, and seated himself there, in order that he might receive them, according to prescribed Oriental etiquette, on the threshold of his dwelling. The first ten men carry large earthen amphoræ full of butter ; then come jars of milk, baskets of eggs, round wicker cages filled with fowls tied by the legs ; four mules laden with loaves of bread, lemons, oranges ; and, finally, twelve sheep, led by the horns—which enter reluctantly, poor beasts, into this foreign camp, as if already their fears misgave them.

There is enough to feed ten caravans such as
ours; but to refuse would show an utter want
of dignity.

Besides, our men, our horsemen, our muleteers
are eyeing this *mouna* with all the greed of
primitive men, eager to partake of it. Throughout the night they will feast upon it; they will
return to it to-morrow; and even then will
leave, scattered on the ground, rich remains
for the wild dogs and jackals. It is a custom
established for centuries : in the camp of an
ambassador one must feast continuously.

. . . .

No sooner has the Minister thanked the
donors (with a simple movement of the head,
as befits a very great chief) than the division
of the spoils begins. At a signal, our men approach; they divide the butter, the loaves,
the eggs; they fill burnouses and hoods, rush
baskets and the pack-saddles of mules. Behind
the kitchen tents, into a little corner of evil
aspect, which, too, is transported with us
every day, they lead the sheep—and they have
to drag them, for the poor beasts understand :
they jib and struggle. In the dying twilight,
almost gropingly, they slaughter them with
ancient knives; the grass in this little corner
runs with their blood. They kill the fowls, too,
in dozens, leaving them to struggle with throat

half-cut, that their flesh may be the whiter. Then fires are kindled all around, for Bedouin cookings that will be worthy of a Pantagruel's feast; little yellow flames leap here and there amid heapings of dry branches, illuminating suddenly groups of camels, groups of mules, which the darkness had already hidden from us; and tall white Arabs who have the air of ghosts. It might be a gipsies' encampment in a time of orgy—in the midst of this desert country spread out in an immense circle around us; which, all at once, as the fires burn up, seems darker and more profound.

The night is overcast, very dark and cold. We are in a region of prairie and marshland. And while the preparations for the feast proceed, crickets, on all sides at once, even in the remote distances, begin for us their nocturnal music, their same eternal concert, which is of all countries and must have been of all the ages of the world.

.　　　.　　　.　　　.　　　.　　　.　　　.

At about eight o'clock, as we are finishing our dinner in the large common tent which serves us for dining-room, the Minister is told that a heifer has just been sacrificed to him; outside, at the door of his own tent. And we go out, lighted by a lantern, to ascertain what this sacrifice portends and who has made it.

It is a Moroccan custom to immolate animals
in this way at the feet of passing chiefs of whom
a favour is to be asked. The victim should lie
a-dying for a long time, shedding its blood little
by little on the ground. If the great one is
disposed to entertain the supplication he accepts
the sacrifice and orders his servants to take up
the slaughtered beast and dispose of it; in the
contrary case, he continues on his way without
turning his head and the disdained offering
remains for the crows. Sometimes, I am told,
when the Sultan travels, the route he has
followed is marked by a trail of carcasses.

The heifer, still living, lies before the Minister's
tent, across the opening; it is breathing heavily,
its nostrils dilated; by the light of the lantern
we can see the large pool of blood which has
issued from its throat and widens slowly on
the grass. And near by are three women—
the suppliants—their arms twined round the
mast of the flag of France.

They are of the neighbouring tribe. During
the first moments of the feasting of our guards,
in the first minutes of famished gluttony, they
had contrived, under cover of the darkness, to
penetrate into the midst of our tents without
being perceived; then, when our men tried to
drive them away, they clung to this flagstaff,
as if they thought they were unassailable under

its protection; and none has dared to remove them by force. They have brought with them four or five little children, who cling to their robes. In the darkness, and with their veils half-lowered, it is not possible to distinguish whether they are young and pretty or ugly and old; their flowing tunics, too, caught up at the shoulder with large plaques of silver which we can see gleaming, conceal all the lines of their bodies.

The interpreter approaches, and other lanterns are brought, illuminating better this group of white forms around a stricken beast which ends by dying on the ground.

They are the three wives of a kaid of the district. For some offence, which it is not for me to judge, their husband has been incarcerated, for two years already, in the prisons of Tangier, at the instance of the French legation. And they want the new French Minister, as a grace of happy advent, to ask his release of the Sultan of Fez.

He may have been very culpable, this kaid —of that I know nothing—but his wives are touching. As well as I can judge that, too, is the opinion of the Minister; and, although he was not willing to make any formal promise on the spot, their cause, it seemed to me, was in way of being gained.

CHAPTER VIII

6th April.

AT about five or six o'clock in the morning, before the sounding of the réveillé, I raise the door of my tent and look outside. And this matutinal appearance of the surrounding country impresses me in an unlooked-for manner.

A sky uniformly dark hangs over the whole of the vast green country in which we are; great plains of irises, of palmetto, of daffodils; in places, patches of white daisies, so thickly growing that they look like drifts of snow; all this wet with rain or dew; in the distance, the intense green turns sombre under heavy, trailing clouds; it turns to the grey of shadow, and, on the horizon, mingles little by little, in gradated planes, with the black of the mountains and the sky—a sinister dawn in a place without a name, lost in the midst of a vast primitive country.

A number of mules, already saddled, thanks to some early risen servants, are grouped in confusion beyond, upright on their legs, but sleeping still. Their high-peaked saddles, covered with ıed cloth, make spots of vivid colour against the neutral-tinted background, against those furthermost planes of inky sky. Motionless there, they look as if they were waiting in readiness for some procession of fairyland without spectators. Our guards, awake, issue one by one from their tents, stretching long brown arms ; having always, by reason of their robes and cloaks, a factitious air of tall, lean old women, of giant gipsies.

And there still are the suppliants of yesterday ! Despite the rain, they have, it seems, passed the night crouched before the tent of the Minister. They are more numerous even, this morning : women, old and young, the whole family of the captive, no doubt, and poor little babies, coiffed in Bedouin fashion, who lie asleep at their mothers' breasts. Near them on the wet grass, at the spot where the heifer was sacrificed, remains a large stain of blood diluted by the rain.

I draw near the group ; and an old tattooed woman, who seems to be the mother of the captive, seizes the flap of my cloak and kisses it. From that moment I am won over to their cause and promise myself to intercede for them when the proper time arrives.

How mournful the place seems, at such an hour as this, mournful and mysterious ! And in the gloomy landscape, how our tents are white !

CHAPTER IX

WE set out like a fantasia, at a gallop, in the cold wind of the morning, almost all abreast, pell-mell, climbing a hill ; and our troop makes a pretty picture, in its medley of uniforms and burnouses, against the green of the hillside. I know not what can have come over the three old negro dolls who guide us, that they make fly so fast the standard of the Sultan ; but our horses, in their freshness, ask nothing better than to follow them, and we no more. And it is joyous and exhilarating, in the early morning, this swiftness, this hurly-burly, this clinking of arms, the whole accompaniment of this rapid flight through good pure air which no one has breathed, which dilates the lungs. Our pack-mules, which, at the start, tried to keep pace with us, are quickly distanced ; some ten or so of them, laden with our cases, come to grief ; then there are cries, yellings of Arabs ; the muleteers, their burnouses streaming, swarm like a cloud of birds of prey upon each fallen beast, to raise it, reload it, thrash it. Vaguely we see these things in our uninterrupted flight.

After all, they are matters which neither concern nor disturb us: the baggage never fails to arrive, and the kaid responsible must look to it. We race on regardless; in the wind, in the rain which begins to streak the air, we continue the movement of our fantasia.

.   .   .   .

When we make an end of our galloping the rain is falling in torrents, and the wind moans, lashing our ears. We are on a rolling plateau, in a region of sand sparsely covered with bracken; before us, as far as we can see, stretch the kinds of dunes of this undulating plain. The sand is of a golden yellow, very fine, and we ride over it noiselessly, as on the floor of a riding-school.

With the prevailing bracken are mingled daffodils, lavender and quantities of white flowers resembling large eglantines. All these plants in the plentiful watering of the rain are deliciously fresh, and, as the hoofs of our horses crush them, give out a sweet fragrance.

Then, for a couple of hours, we traverse a more mournful region, stony, ravined, rugged, with bushes of fragrant furze covered with yellow blossom, and stray hawthorns; an infinity of little wild valleys follow one another, all alike, without sign of humanity. The sky turns darker and darker. The wind screams over the brushwood, the rain stings. It might be a Brittany of yore, before the days of steeples and calvaries ; a prehistoric Brittany, seen in springtime.

The three old negro dolls of our advance guard are coiffed in their pointed hoods. Seen thus from behind, tall and straight on their lean horses, their burnouses spreading over the cruppers, they look like baboons, like conic-shaped baboons, very large of base and tapering to a sharp point. And their red standard, which was new at the setting out, hangs limply now against the mast, soaked and pitiful.

. . . .

We are about to change tribes, so it appears, and to enter the territory of El-Araish. For, beyond, on the brow of a hill, a hundred or so horsemen are awaiting us. Through the blinding rain we perceive them as a quasi-fantastic troop, bristling with long slender guns ; enveloped in white, all of them, their hoods lowered, they neither speak nor move. And it is strange to see them thus, motionless, like mummies, when we know that in a moment a frenzy of swiftness will seize them, and that, in their furious career, the wind will sweep about them a thousand streaming things, burnouses, unrolled turbans, manes and long tails.

On the front of these horsemen, still hooded
and mummied, the kaid advances and offers
his hand to the Minister. He has the face
of a holy prophet, regularly handsome, gentle,
mystical. He wears a caftan of rose-coloured
cloth, with a white and a blue burnous draped
one over the other, and the horse he rides is of
a dappled grey, with trappings of mignonette-
green silk embroidered with gold. His lieutenant who accompanies him, has by contrast
a cruel countenance, with the little hooked
nose of a falcon; mounted on a yellow, blue-
saddled horse, he wears a caftan of nasturtium-
coloured cloth and a slate-coloured burnous.
And such is the light of this country that, even
in this dull rainy weather, the combination of
these colours has a brilliance that no costume
could ever attain under our sky of Europe.

Despite the rain, we must needs assist at the
great fantasia of welcome.

All together the cavaliers throw back their
hoods and spur their horses, which dash forward,
head in air, by furious bounds. Allah ! with
neighings and cries the race is begun, draperies
stream, muskets circle in the air.

Three parts of this " powder play " is in-
effective on account of the torrential rain, and
the kaid is profuse in his excuses, explaining
that the powder is damp. But it is exhilarating

and thrilling, none the less ; perhaps even more extraordinary than under a tranquil blue sky ; frenzied horsemen, lashing rain and dark clouds, all seem driven by the wind in a common whirl.

Amongst this new escort, which will accompany us until to-morrow, are to be seen under the turbans some pairs of eyes that are veritably savage.

.   .   .   .

We call a halt of two hours for luncheon, on a hill where, extraordinary circumstance, is built a village. (It is thanks to these midday halts, we may say, that our tents and cases get ahead of us each day and reach the end of the day's march before us, so that on arrival we find our camp already set up.)

On this hill our men hastily erect the large tent which serves us for dining-room, and, unlike the others, travels always at our own pace, behind us, without losing sight of us. And, as it is very cold, a fire is lit, a veritable bonfire of palm leaves, which burn with a strong balsamic odour, and emit a smoke of conflagration.

The village that is here is composed, like those of yesterday, of little huts of grey thatch hidden behind hedges of large aloes and bluish cacti. Near by is a date-palm, straight and slender of stem, the first we have met with since our departure. There is also the tomb of a holy marabout, greatly venerated in the district; a white flag floats above it, indicating to travellers, to the caravans, that it behoves them to stay their passing and place piously there an offering of money. (In Morocco there are many holy tombs marked thus by a white flag, even in the most uninhabited and solitary places, and the gifts of the infrequent wayfarers are generally respected by thieves.)

. . . .

While we were lunching on the remains of yesterday's *mouna*, the weather has become fine again; with the rapidity peculiar to Africa, the sky, quickly swept clear of cloud, has resumed its wonderful blue transparency; the light has reappeared magnificent.

In this treeless country one can see to extreme distances; besides, there is scarce ever house or village or anything to break the immense green or brown monotony; thus the eye becomes accustomed to sweep the great line of the horizon, to discover at once, as on the plains of the sea, anything unusual that happens there, anything that is an indication of movement or of life, even at distances at which, in our countries, one could distinguish nothing. When, on the side of a hill, bluish in the distance, white dots appear we come to know, if they remain stationary, that they are stones; if they move about, that they are sheep. A group of reddish spots indicates a herd of cattle; and a long brown trail, advancing with undulating slowness, crawling like a caterpillar, ceaselessly, tranquilly, straightway represents for us a caravan, and we imagine that we can distinguish the long line of camels, rocking their long necks in sleepy oscillation.

An extraordinary object which has accompanied us from Tangier and which we have grown used to seeing, sometimes ahead of us, sometimes behind us, in the distance, is an electric launch, some twenty feet in length, which we are taking as a present to his Majesty the Sultan. It is enclosed in a shell of greyish wood and has the appearance of a block of granite; and it proceeds slowly, through the ravines, over the mountains, borne on the shoulders of two score Arabs. One may see huge things of the kind in the Egyptian bas-reliefs, carried, like this, by trains of white-robed, bare-legged men.

.   .   .   .

We camp to-night at a place called Tlata-Raissana, where, I am told, an immense market of beasts and slaves is held every month.

But to-day the place is deserted. It lies on the bank of a large, strongly flowing stream,

amid mountains so carpeted with bracken that
they seem to be covered with a kind of fleecy
material, of a wonderful green. There is, as
always, a quantity of flowers around our
tents, but they are no longer the flowers of
France; here, in this particular spot, on the
heather - clad earth, grow species unknown
to our countryside or in our gardens; very
fragrant, all of them, and coloured a little
strangely.

Fantasias gallop around our camp throughout the evening; until the setting of the sun
we hear nothing but the noise of horses thunder-
ing past, gun-shots, and shouts of Arabs.

. . . .

About seven o'clock the *mouna* makes its
entry into the camp with customary majesty.
But it is inadequate : no more than eight sheep,
and other things in proportion. It is beneath
acceptance by an embassy, and must be refused
in order to maintain the dignity of our flag.
And this refusal constitutes a diplomatic
incident, which might become a very serious
matter for the kaid of the district, if it came to
the ears of the Sultan.

He feigns surprise and consternation, with
delicious gestures, the handsome pink-robed
kaid. He pretends to lay the blame on kaids
of less degree, who in turn lay the blame on

their subordinates, who start belabouring with sticks the innocent shepherds.

But it was nothing but a comedy which they had planned together to put us to the proof ; a complementary *mouna* was in readiness to meet eventualities, hidden a little distance away in a ravine. After we have supped, a new procession appears in the moonlight, bringing this time sixteen sheep, a respectable number of fowls, of loaves and jars of butter. And the kaids, anxious to hear what the Minister may say, wait in silence around the tent, in the majesty of their long white burnouses. This new *mouna*, in all respects suitable, is accepted, and the incident is closed.

CHAPTER X

HAVING crossed, beneath a sky still lowering and dark, the first of the surrounding mountains, clothed with velvety bracken, we find ourselves once more in endless solitudes, full white with flowering daffodils.

Here and there, a tall red gladiole, or a cluster of purple irises, fly their beautiful fresh colours in the midst of the monotonous whiteness of this flower garden. And so it is as far as eye can see.

Ever and anon, storks pass in slow flight, beating the air with large bipartite wings of white and black; and crows also, and eagles.

Ceaselessly it rains. And there is no one in sight, this morning—not a group of peasants, not a file of donkeys, not a caravan.

A mother camel, alone with her little son by the side of the ill-marked track, approaches with an air of interest to watch us file past. Her baby son, who, I think, can be but newly born, has a neck so slender, and a head so small, that, in the distance, he looks like a four-footed ostrich. The little fellow is almost

46

winning, in his naïve astonishment at sight of us, in his babyish, startled grace.

And still it rains, rains in torrents. Our three old negro dolls of the advance guard, their hoods drawn down over their eyes to-day, look more than ever like pointed monkeys. The silk standard, which the midmost doll holds ever straight as a taper, is nothing better than a discoloured rag, tattered by the wind. The water streams from us all. And the Sultan's launch, always like some accessory of an Egyptian procession, advances with the utmost difficulty, the feet of its forty bearers sinking at each step into the sodden ground.

After travelling for two hours through this prairie of daffodils, we notice something like a very long fissure serpentining in the plain, something that bids fair to be a river with very steep banks.

It is the Oued M'Cazen, reputed difficult to cross, and on its banks is an assemblage of unhappy augury: laden mules in hundreds, camels, horsemen, pedestrians, all brought to a stop there, evidently because the river is not fordable.

The Oued, swollen by the rains, is turbulent, rapid, rolls noisily its muddy waters, which seem, truly, to be of great depth. It flows, too, between high vertical banks of clayey

earth, sodden, slippery, absolutely dangerous.
With our European notions of travel, it would
seem to us practically impossible, without some
sort of bridge, to get our men, our baggage and
tents, across it.

Our kaids, however, are of a different opinion,
and are going to make the attempt, venturing
first that which is of least consequence.

First, our serving men, who, in a trice, take
off their burnouses, all their handsome draperies
of grey wool, bare their graceful brown bodies
and plunge into the cold and tormented water
to try the depth : six feet at most ; with a
little good will the thing might perhaps be
done.

Let us try now some lightly burdened
mules.

Encouraged by blows, they enter the water
and swim towards the middle ; are bewildered
for a minute in the current, which sweeps them
along ; then quickly feel their feet on the mud
of the farther bank, with their load complete,
though soaked with muddy water.

But how are we to cross, whose ambassadorial
dignity prevents us from disrobing ? And our
mattresses ? And our elegant uniforms with
their facings of gold, which are to figure before
the Sultan at the presentation ?

On the height of the opposite bank a small

troop of horsemen arrives at a gallop, shouting lustily, and making signs to us. We are saved! It is one Shaoush of Czar-el-Kebir (a town we are approaching), who has come to our assistance, with a numerous suite, bringing a *mahadia* constructed in haste against our need. (A *mahadia* is a kind of sheaf, an enormous bundle of reeds, bound together in such fashion as to float.) Two at a time we embark on this improvised raft ; by a rope we are hauled across ; and our cases, our precious luggage, cross in the same manner, dry as in a boat.

As for the rest of our column, men and beasts, they have to swim, all of them, and as quickly as may be. The kaids bustle about, shouting, calling to one another at the top of their voices, always with those raucous aspirations which sound like the suffocations of fury : " 'Ha! Kaid Rhaa!—'Ha! Kaid Abder-Haman!— 'Ha! Kaid Kaddour!" And, right and left, they fall to beating with their sticks the waverers whom the cold water daunts.

Resignedly, the handsome Arab horsemen disrobe, then unharness their horses too, and remount them, holding them forked between their strong limbs as in a vice of bronze. On their own heads they place in a monumental pile their caftans and their burnouses ; above that again, their enormous high-peaked saddle,

D

their gaily coloured harness; and then raise their arms, like the handles of a Grecian amphora, to support the whole.

Then we see advancing resolutely towards the river all these multi-coloured scaffoldings, incomprehensible at first sight, having each for its base this unstable thing: a lean little horse, rearing and restive, at the sides of which hang two long bare legs.

And all these men, laden in this way, unable now to use their hands, set their horses at the perpendicular and slippery bank, by mere pressure of their knees, using their heels as spurs. The horses neigh with fear; slide, like one who skates, like one who toboggans, some still upright on their legs, others on their haunches, and, all covered with sticky mud, plunge into the Oued with a great splashing of water; then swim in midstream and, on the hither bank, climb like goats.

Out of the quantity there are a few that fall, that struggle, that kick; there are horsemen who are thrown into the river, with their bright folded burnouses, their handsome saddles, which in their top-heaviness drag them down. Some of the mules falter in distress in the mud: they are urged on by cries and blows, horribly wrung by the girths and pack-saddles, their flesh all raw; and the tents they carry, so white at the setting out, are now smothered in mud.

In the midst of this immense grassy plain, under this lowering sky, on these banks of grey earth, it is a strange sight, the activity, the business, of some hundred horses and horsemen of all varieties of colour, of as many mules, camels, pedestrians and serving-men. We have the appearance of an emigrant tribe, hastening as in a flight after rout.

The situation is now complicated by a herd of oxen, which is swimming across in a direction opposite to that of our caravan—stubborn oxen that wanted to remain on the other bank. The Arabs driving them struggle with them in the water, swimming with one arm, beating them with the other, now twisting their tails to hasten their progress, now dragging them by the horns.

Towards the finish, the clayey earth of the banks is polished like a veritable mirror by the successive slippings. Then the crossing becomes a kind of catastrophe, a general downfall, to the accompaniment of furious cries; an immense confusion of maddened beasts, of naked men, of baggage of every sort, of red saddles, of packages wrapped in gaudy coverings—a scene such as must have come to pass at the time of the invasion of the armies of the

Prophet. It is a grand picture of ancient Africa, admirable in its colour and animation, in the midst of desert plains, under a black sky.

At length 'tis a thing accomplished, brought, by dint of blows and shoutings, to a happy issue. We are all, with our baggage, on the farther bank, without drownings, without loss; our cases, our mattresses, soaked and covered with mud; our mules sore and breathless; ourselves, wet with rain only.

And the desert of daffodils and irises begins again, tranquil and mournful in the downpour, for another hour. Our troop is swelled by the men from Czar-el-Kebir, who came to meet us, brought by Shaoush : ten Arabs on horseback, and as many long-haired Jews, wearing large gold earrings and mounted two by two on donkeys. Czar-el-Kebir, the town at which we shall arrive this evening, is the only one between Tangier and Fez; and Shaoush, a handsome Arab in an amaranth burnous, is our Consular Agent there. If I am asked what we do with a Consular Agent at Czar-el-Kebir, the answer is that we have there some French protégés—twenty, perhaps; as, for that matter, at Tangier and Tetuan also. In the majority of the Mussulman towns of Turkey, of Syria and Egypt, we have, in the same way, a number of these protégés—that is to say, people whom it is not permissible to touch without the consent of our legations.   In Morocco, almost all our protégés are Israelites —why, I have never been able to ascertain.

We continue on our way, then, in this plain of white flowers.   Innumerable swallows, skimming the earth, pass between the legs of our horses.

From time to time we encounter flocks of sheep.   The shepherd or shepherdess is a little heap of grey wool with a pointed hood, huddled on the grass in the rain.   As we pass, the burnous straightens, stands fully upright, to enjoy the astonishing spectacle of our caravan on the march.   Then, under the tattered covering, a childish figure is disclosed, half-naked, slim and yellow.   The face is nearly always refined and charming, with white teeth and large black eyes.

Towards evening, we enter a cultivated region, a region quite commonplace, recalling the plains of Beauce, but immensely enlarged, without houses or enclosures ; cornfields and cornfields and barley-fields without end ; the soil, black and rich, must be marvellously fertile.   What a granary of abundance this Morocco might become !

On an elevation that bounds the view in front of us appears an unexpected thing, a thing we have been unaccustomed to see, a human crowd—an Arab crowd, a crowd in burnouses and uniformly grey, undulating against the grey background of the sky. It is the population of Czar, which has come out to meet us. Men on foot, men on horseback, all with hoods lowered and forming rows of pointed silhouettes. We can hear already the beating of the drums and the wailing of the bagpipes.

As soon as we are within range, all the long guns, loaded with powder, are discharged at us, and the horsemen rush forward like a fantasia, while the music, in furious crescendo, sends us its most harrowing notes. Then, by a turning movement, the crowd envelops us, mingles with us, penetrates us, in confusion, in tumult, the beasts jostling and biting one another. The horsemen trot, the pedestrians run, burnouses in the wind, harassed by the horses, under a continual menace of destruction. There are numbers of children on donkeys, sometimes two or three on a single beast, looking comically skewered; there are old men on crutches; there are halt, who nevertheless contrive to run; there are beggars and idiots and visionary holy men a-singing. And the tabour players, who are on foot, beat their hardest, terrifying our horses. And the pipers, who are on mule-back, their cheeks swollen like the bladders of

their screeching pipes, their eyes starting out
of their head, pipe and pipe enough to burst
their veins, urging on their restive mounts by
digs of their bare feet. One of these pipers,
round as a ball, with an enormous head, pot-
bellied on a little donkey, resembles some old
Silenus; he follows me obstinately, making
his bagpipe yelp in my ears with a kind of rage,
like the mournful cry of a jackal. They shout
with all their might: " Hou ! " in a drawling,
mournful falsetto. " Hou ! Allah send victorious our Sultan Mulai-Hassan ! Hou ! "

Our horses, very excited, very restive, prance
in time to the rhythm of the tabours, and we
proceed thus towards Czar, deafened by unfamiliar music, in a frenzy of noise.

Czar is disclosed little by little, blurred at
first in the rain. In the midst of a plain as
fertile as the Promised Land, it is surrounded
by a wood of olives and orange-trees, magnificently green. It has not the whiteness of
Arab towns; on the contrary, it is of an earthy
colour, and its fifteen or twenty minarets,
which are of a dull brown, resemble in the distance the steeples of our countries of the north ;
under this cloudy sky, and in these flooded
meadows, you might imagine that you were
arriving at a Flemish town. It needs the
few slender palm-trees, very high in the stem,

that sway above, to give the impression of
Africa.

But this impression soon becomes definite
enough when we see, in the old, crumbling
ramparts, the exquisite ogival gateways framed
with arabesques.

On the side of a hill, some two hundred yards
from the walls, in an abandoned cemetery,
where the old tombs are covered with golden-
yellow lichen, we find our little camp in course
of being got ready. Our tents, our mattresses,
our baggage, still lie upon the grass, soaked
with rain. 'Tis a pitiful spectacle, like the
unpacking of a showman in winter.

.   .   .   .

Over and above the *mouna* that is due to us,
there are brought to us to-night, by courtesy,
numerous dishes, all prepared and hot. It is
the occasion, too, of the first appearance in our
camp of a kind of utensil with which, so we are
told, we shall be called upon to make familiar
acquaintance in the banquets of Fez: an
enormous round box, surmounted by a cover,
a roof, rather, in the form of a tall cone, made
of coloured esparto grass. At banquets of state
the dishes are always brought in under these
coverings, and are carried on the heads of the
servants. At nightfall ten grave personages
arrive before us, coiffed all with these extra-

ordinary things, to which their bare, upraised arms make, as it were, handles; and without a word they deposit them on the ground, before the tent of the Minister.

Under these esparto roofings are large earthenware tubs, filled with viands heaped up in pyramids; a sweet couscous; a savoury couscous, crowned with an edifice of chickens; a roasted sheep; and a pile of those highly spiced tarts known in Morocco as " gazelles' hoofs."

We partake of all these good things under our tent in the evening; our little table is hidden beneath the monstrous dishes; we might be supping with Pantagruel And on our leavings the men will afterwards make feast till daybreak. To-morrow there will remain nothing of these mountains of viands; it is difficult to realise what Arabs, at ordinary times so moderate, are capable of devouring, when Destiny has marked them out to escort an embassy.

CHAPTER XI

THE trumpet does not sound the réveillé in our camp this morning; which means that we are held up by the rain—that the river of Czar-el-Kebir (the Oued Leucoutz) is, as we feared, impassable.

We rise, therefore, later than usual, having slept beneath a wet tent, above wet ground, between wet blankets.

The tabours and the bagpipes are already to be heard. Throughout the morning musicians, sorcerers and fools roam about our camp; and poor, too, of both sexes, gathering the discarded claws of fowls, the bones of sheep, all the debris of our orgy, on the sodden ground of this cemetery.

After breakfast, in a lull of the rain, we mount our horses to go to inspect the ford, the im-passable ford of the river. Escorted always by our guards, and preceded by the red standard, we proceed towards the town, which we have to traverse in its greatest length. (Despite the undoubted warmth of our welcome, despite the presents and the smiles, we follow the advice of the wise, which warns us never to venture forth without escort, never to walk alone more than a hundred yards from the tents ; such, indeed, is the recommendation of the Sultan himself, who fears for his Christian guests the misguided zeal of fanatics.)

The road leading to the town is a sink of liquid mud, littered with large stones and putre- fying carcasses. We gallop over it none the less, since such is the custom ; in Morocco one never hesitates to adopt this movement of parade, even on pathways on which, at home, one would fear to walk a led horse. Outside the still standing walls, hidden under cacti, under reeds and wild oats, are quantities of debris of ramparts dating back I know not to what uncertain epochs. Czar-el-Kebir, so ignored to-day, can boast a past of most varied experience. It was from here long ago that expeditions of holy war went forth to the con- quest of Spain. Some centuries later, after the fall of Granada, the town, taken and retaken, destroyed and rebuilt an incalculable number of times, fell into the hands of the Portuguese, and about three hundred years ago, following the " Battle of the Three Emperors," it became again definitively Moroccan. Since then it has slept and slowly crumbled, in the midst of its exquisite gardens.

We enter through a series of old ogival gateways, tramping always in puddles of sticky mud, which the hoofs of our horses send in spurts against the walls. All is sombre and sinister to-day in these dripping ruins. Each little street, narrow and tortuous, is a sewer, a filthy stream, from which our passage releases noxious vapours. We meet none but men hooded in dirty white, clothed in grey rags, their legs bare, yellow and muddy. They make way for us, sheltering in doorways to avoid our splashing, and eye us with indifference ; their faces, for the most part handsome, have an indescribable air of gloom and mystery; deep in their souls they cherish an old religious dream which we are no longer able to understand. But they, evidently, are not the people who greeted us yesterday in the fields, musicians at their head ; I know not where they may have recruited those manifesters of welcome; these folk here have not curiosity enough to look at us.

One feels from the first that the town is not of Arab construction ; it is not white, and its sloping roofs are covered with tiles ; the whole is of a sombre grey overgrown with golden-yellow moss, and has an air of decrepit antiquity. It was built by the Portuguese, and the Arabs on arrival found it such as it is. Only here and there they have carved their denticulated

porticoes, their inimitable ogives. And they
have built their mosques, their high square
towers for the chanting of the prayers, their tall
minarets on which the motionless storks find a
resting-place. But the white chalk could take
no hold on these foreign, unfaced walls; and
so they left them their nondescript colour.

In the bazaar, which is covered and dark,
the passages are so narrow that our horses, in
single file, brush against the stalls. The traders,
seated in their little niches, seem detached from
the commerce of this world and careless of
buyers. Their wares consist for the most part
of leather goods, gay trappings for horses, and
multi-coloured rush-mats which are hung in
thick variegated bunches on every side.

Then comes the Jewish quarter, at least as
large as that of the Arabs. Here you might
imagine yourself in Turkey, or Syria, or
Egypt; the Jews are alike in each and all of
the Mussulman countries. Their faces, their
costumes, their horses, almost everything that
is theirs, are copied from the same invariable
models.

We leave the town by other ogives, warped
and wry, but always beautified by delicate
figurings and framings. And here is the river,
the Oued Leucoutz (the ancient Leucus of the
Romans). It is larger than that of yesterday,

and even more steeply banked, Its muddy waters roll swiftly, noisily by. Some of our men undress and dive to ascertain its depths. Ten or twelve feet! We must give up the attempt for to-day. There is, it seems, an old ferry-boat in the vicinity and instructions are given to hasten its repair and to hold it in readiness.

We return to the town, where we are invited to two collations, one at the house of Shaoush and the other at the house of a certain sherif, whose father, a Court jester, was a favourite of a late sultan.

The receptions at the houses of these two personages are much alike. Dismounting our horses before little festooned doors, which scarcely open, very narrow, very low, in high decrepit walls, we are introduced into interior courts, colonnaded, and paved and panelled with mosaics. There we are sprinkled with rose-water, flung as one uses a whip full in our face from silver bottles very long and slender in the neck; pieces of precious Indian wood are kindled in brasiers in our honour, shedding a thick odorous smoke; then we are offered " gazelles' hoofs," in large dishes, and tea in microscopic cups, as in China—tea which is brewed on the ground in silver samovars, and is very sweet, and strongly flavoured with mint, anise and cinnamon. Coffee is scarcely ever taken in Morocco—tea always and everywhere. And it comes from England, as do also the samovars in which it is made and the gilded cups from which it is drunk. English ships unload at the open ports considerable quantities of these things and the caravans carry them afterwards into the very heart of Al Moghreb.

The reception of the sherif, the son of the Court jester, seems to me, however, the more interesting of the two, and his house, also; his old house, with its mosaics and its whitenesses, immense and ruinous. He is himself of a strange and attractive personality. His face, extremely refined and gentle, preserves an expression constantly mystical; at every courteous word we venture to speak to him he crosses his hands upon his heart, in a pose of the saints of the Primitives, and bows his head with the smile of a girl.

I linger in his company at the very top of his house, on his terrace, which is large as a public square and warped and cracked by rain and sun; layers of whitewash, accumulated in the course of centuries, have rounded all its angles; it is bordered by a crenellated wall, with little loopholes through which one may see afar off without being seen. It is the highest promenade of the town; and from it one commands a view of the whole. Alone, the sombre old towers of the mosques, with their immobile storks, reach higher into the sky. Contrary to custom though it be, it is here, he says, that he passes the greater part of his life, above all his summer evenings. For political reasons he was expelled from Fez while still a child, and has no hope of obtaining the grace ever to quit this residence at Czar-el-Kebir, which has been assigned to him by the Sultan as a place of exile. He studies the sciences and philosophy, as they were taught, no doubt, in the Middle Ages, in priceless old Arab manuscripts, in which divination and alchemy hold a large place.

There are three of us here, making in pensive mood the tour of this high terrace: he, the sherif, clothed all in white robes; Shaoush, in long violet caftan, and I—and I feel, uneasily, that I am a blot in this ageless picture, which, were I not there, might well be dated from the year 1200, or even the year 1000. I think of the depths of tranquillity and mysticism that must separate the conceptions of this sherif from those of a gentleman of the boulevards; I try to imagine what his imprisoned life can be, his dream, his hope, and I envy him those summer evenings of which he spoke to me, passed here in contemplating from above all these other terraces of the dead town, in listening to the sing-song of the prayers, in scanning the wild distances of the plain and of the surrounding mountains; in watching, along these tracks by which no carriage has ever travelled, the passing of the caravans.

.   .   .   .

Returning in the rain to our camp, splashed from head to foot with the fetid water of the streets and sewers, we find the approaches to our tents more than ever overrun by the vagrants of Czar. Sorcerers, again, and beggars without legs, who have dragged themselves hither on their stumps through the thick mud, in the hope of picking up a few bronze *floucs* (little coins, bearing the seal of Solomon, of which it needs about seven to equal a sou). Some old women, half naked, are on all-fours, under our mules, scratching the earth with their nails, to find the grains that remain of the barley and oats.

CHAPTER XII

9th April.

HEAVY rain and high wind throughout the night. In our tents there is nothing that is dry.

Once more the réveillé sounds under a black sky. We mount our horses, nevertheless, determined to cross the river at all hazards and continue our journey.

With our whole escort, this time, with all our train of camels and mules, we have to pass again through Czar, to enter by the same old festooned gates, to thread the same dark little mousetrap streets, to splash through the same puddles, the same mud, the same refuse.

On the farther side of the town, at the gate by which we leave, an old woman who thinks we do not understand her pretends to be a beggar praying for the prosperity of our journey, and holding out her hand for alms cries to us: " God curse your religion ! Curse it ! Curse it !

" Curse it ! Curse it ! " She rocks herself to the rhythm of her song, in apt imitation of the supplicating poor, and her old mocking voice swells, when we have passed, in pursuit of us.

We make a somewhat long detour, in a neighbourhood of gardens and orchards, in order to
approach the river at a more convenient spot,
where the repaired ferry-boat is awaiting us.

And what marvellous gardens they are!
Groves of orange-trees shedding a surpassing
fragrance; palm-trees and large arborescent
blue-foliaged cacti and red geraniums; pomegranate-trees, fig-trees and olive-trees, all of
the wonderful green of spring, of the tender
green of April. In the exuberant luxuriance
of this vegetation, the plants of Europe are
mingled with those of Africa; amongst the aloes
are tall blue borages covered with blossom;
acanthi, their foliage streaked with white, grow
in profusion, rising to a height of eight or
ten feet; hemlocks and fennels overtop the
heads of our horses, and the old walls, and the
palisades, are tapestried with bindweed and
periwinkle.

Looking back, we can still see above the
trees the high grey towers of the distant
mosques; in this kind of enchanted grove, their
heads, upraised as if to watch us, suffice to
preserve the ever sombre impression of Islam.
The tracks we follow are foul sewers, with
which nothing in our countries can compare;
our horses sink to the knees in a sort of greasy
pulp; often they stumble on the skull of an

ox, on the carcass of a dog, on a shin-bone;
and at every step—splosh, splosh—the black
mud flies.

Gold-hammers and chaffinches sing at the top
of their voices in the branches, storks come
and settle on one leg on the tops of the trees to
watch us pass. And, at intervals, giving access
to the shady enclosures, open ancient little
ogival doors, ornamented with festoons, with
stalactites, exquisite still in their last decrepitude, under their shroud of white chalk,
with their crowns of climbing roses and red
geraniums. And the orange-trees overtop
everything with their enormous blossomed
tufts; the air is saturated utterly with their
suave perfume.

The river Leucoutz hurries its waters along
with the same impetuosity as yesterday, and
seems even more swollen than before. But the
ferry-boat, set afloat again, is there, and we are
going to cross, a few at a time, as at the Oued
M'Cazen, leaving the greater number of our
men and all our horses to swim.

A crowd has followed us out of the town,
consisting mainly of Jews, who are without
prejudice. The high bank is soon crowned with
human heads amongst the reeds, and children,
to see better, climb the trees.

Then the great scene is repeated; a clamour,

intermittent at first, rises from our escort ; then swells rapidly, becomes general, frenzied.

These cries, accompanied with thwackings and strugglings, are naturally necessary to the loading of the ferry-boat, which has to make an incalculable number of crossings. And, at last, when the load is complete for one journey, when the boat is laden with men and chattels, and the kaid, by dint of furious imprecations, has succeeded in getting it pushed off, all the men on board, for the sake of joining in the outcry, give voice to another kind of roar, in unison this time and long drawn-out ; something that sounds like a cry of triumph, as much as to say, " We depart, we float, we cleave the waters."

The horses struggle : the plunge into the rapid and cold water has no attraction for them. The camels, too, sway their long necks, crying, groaning, The mules above all, stubborn by nature, refuse absolutely to budge. And sometimes eight or ten Arabs at a time are leagued against a single obstinate beast, which throws back its ears, and neighs and kicks, its hide all scored with the pressure of the pack-saddle, its flesh raw and bleeding. In a shower, in cadence, the blows descend on the luckless beast's quarters, which resound like a drum.

On the farther shore, with our escort of a
hundred horsemen, sabre at side and gun on
shoulder, we re-form our long column in fields
of luxuriant corn and barley, which make
velvety carpets of most enchanting green.
We trample the goodly growth underfoot, but
in Morocco that does not matter, there is more
in plenty; wheat fetches but three francs a
quintal, and no one husbands it; if they but
knew, indeed, in the season, how to store the
harvests, there would be an end to famine in
the land, and the poor would have no need
to come, as yesterday, to gather the grains
rejected by the mules. The sun, which has
reappeared, is burning; without transition, the
heat has become overpowering, under a sky
that shows great rents of blue. Czar-el-Kebir
disappears behind us, with its orange groves,
its lovely gardens, its mud, its stenches and its
perfumes.

.   .   .   .

About midday, once more in wild solitary
country, we pitch our dining tent in a delightful spot, of uttermost fragrance. It is in the
hollow of a green valley that has no name,
where springs spurt on all sides from between
mossy stones, where small clear streams run
amongst myosotis and watercress and anemones. The sky, now wholly blue, is of an

infinite clearness; we are reminded of those
glorious noontides of the month of June at
the time of haymaking. No trees anywhere,
nothing but these carpets of flowers; as far
as the view extends, incomparable patterns on
the plain; but the expression, a "carpet of
flowers," has been so abused in application to
ordinary meadows that it has lost the force
needed for description here: zones absolutely
pink with large mallows; marblings white as
snow, which are masses of daisies; streaks of
magnificent yellow, which are trails of butter-
cups. Never, in any garden, in any artificial
English flower bed, have I seen such a luxuriance of flowers, such a packed grouping of the
same kinds, giving together such vivid colours.
The Arabs must have been inspired by their
desert prairies in the weaving of those carpets
of fine wool, diapered with bright and striking
colours, that are made at Rabat and at Mogador.
And the hillsides, where the earth is dryer, are
draped with another and different kind of
finery; there it is the kingdom of lavender;
of lavender so closely growing, flowering so
uniformly to the exclusion of every other plant,
that the ground is absolutely violet, with an
ashy violet, a powdered violet; it is as if the
hillside were covered with some softly tinted
plush; and the contrast with the frank bril-

liance of the prairie is striking. As we tread
the lavender underfoot, a strong healthy perfume escapes from the bruised stalks, impregnates our clothing, impregnates the air. And
butterflies in thousands, beetles, flies, and little
winged creatures of divers sorts, circle about,
buzzing, intoxicated with the fragrance and the
light. In our paler countries of the north, or
in the countries of the tropics enervated by
continual heat, there is nothing to equal the
splendour of such a spring.

.   .   .   .

Early in the afternoon's march we return to
a boundless region of white daffodils, which
continues till the evening.

At about two o'clock we quit the territory of
El-Araish and enter that of the Sefiann. As
always, on the boundary of the new tribe, two
or three hundred horsemen await us, drawn up in
line, their straightened guns glinting in the sun.

As soon as they are in sight, those who have
been escorting us from Czar gallop ahead and
range themselves in line, facing the others;
we file then between these two columns; and,
in proportion as we pass, there is a movement
behind us on right and left, and the two lines
close, mingle and follow us.

The place where this happens is a wilderness
of flowers, as entrancing as the most marvellous

of gardens; amongst the white distaffs of the daffodils, are scattered, here and there, tall red gladioli and large purple irises; our horses are breast-high in flowers; we could gather them in sheaves without dismounting, by merely stretching out a hand. And the whole plain is the same, with never a human vestige, bounded on the horizon by a girdle of wild mountains.

The long stalks of the flowers bending before our passage make a light noise, like the rustling of silk.

The sky is clouded once more, but with a fairy gauze; it is like a tissue of little dappled clouds of dove-grey, which seem to have climbed prodigiously high into the ether. After the heavy clouds, low and dark, which for the last few days have poured their showers upon us, it is a delight to travel under this tranquil vault, which sifts a light of exceeding softness, and leaves the horizon profoundly clear. The distances of this immense garden in which we journey this evening are coloured with the tints of Eden.

And throughout our march, which lasts for another two hours, the fantasias continue without a pause.

First, all the horsemen gallop ahead to a great distance—two or three hundred horse-

men. Very strange they look, seen thus from
behind, in their pointed hoods and the uniform
whiteness of their trailing cloaks. We do not
see their horses, which are buried, hidden in
the herbage and flowers; almost unaccountable
they seem, these men in long veils, fleeing with
the swiftness of a dream; and somehow, this
gentle spring sky, and the whiteness of their
costumes, amid all these white flowers, awaken
vaguely recollections of religious processions,
of convent feast days, of the " Month of
Mary."

Suddenly, all together, they turn about; then
we see the bronze faces of the men and the
ruffled heads of the horses, and all the brilliant
colours of the caftans and saddles. At a hoarse
word of command, given by the kaids, they
return at full speed, abreast in little batches,
bearing down upon us at an infernal gallop.
Brrr!... brrr!... On either side of our column
they pass, upright in their stirrups, the reins
dropped on the horses' necks, twirling their
muskets in the air, at the height of naked arms
outstretched from burnouses that stream in
the wind. And every horseman of every group,
at the moment of passing us, shouts his war-
cry, fires his gun, then hurls it into the void and
with one hand recovers it in his flight. Scarce
have we had time to look at them than others

follow, and then others, and others, as in the endless processions of the theatre. Brrr ! . . . brrr ! . . . thunderously they pass, with always the same hoarse cries, always the same noise of daffodils bending and breaking as before the wind of a hurricane.

These Sefiann are by far the most handsome and the most numerous horsemen we have met with since our departure from Tangier.

We are to camp to-night near the dwelling of their chief, the Kaid Ben-Aouda, whose little white blockhouse, in its garden of orange-trees, we can see beyond in the midst of the desert of flowers. Our camp is there, too, pitched, in the familiar circle, on a high prairie of fine grass, on a kind of esplanade overlooking the solitudes; and around the tents a hedge of cacti, as tall as trees, makes for us a park-like enclosure.

The *mouna* of the Kaid Ben-Aouda is superb, brought to the feet of the Minister by the usual train of grave Bedouins, clothed all in white : twenty sheep, innumerable fowls, amphoræ filled with a thousand things, a sugar-loaf for each of us, and, bringing up the rear, four faggots to make us fires. (In this treeless country this present is altogether regal.)

Then, as if there was not already enough, at about eight o'clock in the evening, in the clear blue moonlight, we see arriving a slow and

silent procession, fifty snow-white robes, bearing
on their heads those huge esparto things of
which I have already spoken, resembling the
gables of turrets; fifty dishes of couscous,
arranged in pyramids, and all ready, all cooked,
all hot. At the moment when I am about to
repair to my tent, my eyes heavy with sleep, I
see, as through a fantastic veil, this last picture
of the day: the fifty dishes of couscous arranged in a perfect circle on the grass, ourselves
in the middle; beyond, in a second circle, the
carriers, in their long white robes, in line as if to
dance a round; beyond them again our white
tents, forming a third and wider circle; then
the vast horizon, vague and bluish, surrounding
all; and, in the very middle of the heavens, the
moon—a troubled moon, a moon of vision, a
phantom of a moon—with an immense white
halo, which seems the reflection, in the sky, of
all these circles of terrestrial things.

I fall asleep to the song of the night watch,
which has been instructed to-night to keep a
specially sharp look-out for nocturnal attacks.
To their voices, which are prolonged and drawn
out over the empty prairie, reply from afar
off the doleful cries of jackals, the first that we
have heard since our entry into Morocco—oh!
nothing worth speaking about: two or three
little muted cries just to tell us, as it were:

"We are here"; but there is something about them so mysteriously mournful that we feel our marrow freeze at this mere warning of proximity.

.   .   .   .

Beneath my tent I sleep a sleep of a peculiar kind; which is absolute and yet not heavy; which is restful and nevertheless traversed by dreams—dreams which are rather furtive reflexes of physical sensations; dreams very incomplete, such as animals might dream. Brrr! . . . I seem to hear the dull echo of a flight of Arab horsemen brushing past me in the night; then I have the impression that I myself am being borne along at a gallop, the illusion of swiftness, the resurgence and the reaction of some unnoticed jerking I had suffered during the day; and, again, my arm stiffens quickly in the instinctive movement of checking a stumbling horse. During these confused recoltions of physical life the grand pure air from outside passes over my head. And the nights of sleep, begun at a very early hour, end most often as soon as the day breaks.

CHAPTER XIII

10th April.

I AM awakened by cries—horrible cries—quite near me; a kind of vile belching which seems to issue from some monstrous gullet suffocating with fury. It is already daylight, alas! and the trumpet will soon sound the réveillé, for all the black arabesques that decorate the exterior of my dwelling are revealed in the transparency of the stretched canvas which is infiltrated with golden light. And these same rays of the rising sun outline in fantastic shadow on my wall the form of the beast responsible for these hideous cries : a long, long neck that twists like a caterpillar, and, at its extremity, a small, flattened head with hanging lips : a camel. I knew it indeed at once from the horrible voice : a fool of a camel, restive or in distress.

I watch the movement of its silhouette with the greatest uneasiness. Confusion! What I feared has happened; the beast has caught its feet in the ropes of my tent, and struggles now, and bellows its hardest, shaking the whole tent, which threatens momentarily to collapse upon my head. Then I hear the camel-driver running up calling : " Ts ! Ts ! Ts ! " (That is what is said to the camels to calm them, and, generally, they are amenable to the argument.)

Again : " Ts ! Ts ! Ts ! " The camel is quietened and led away. My tent becomes motionless again, and I fall asleep for a few minutes more.

The trumpet sounds the réveillé, gay and clear ! Quickly as always we arise. Make a hurried breakfast of black bread and *mouna* butter full of red hairs and impurities, while our camp is being dismantled. Then the signal to saddle and we are off !

Our carpet of flowers this morning is composed, at first, of large blue convolvuli mixed with red anemones. Then come sandy plains where a few rare daffodils are still to be seen, burnt and pitiful ; yellowish expanses which have already a Saharan aspect.

We are approaching a place called Seguedla, where every Wednesday is held an immense market more frequented even than that of Tlata-Raissana, which we passed the day before yesterday. People come to it, we are told, from twenty to thirty miles around.

And in the distance, in the midst of this country without villages, without houses, without trees, in the distance, two or three low hills

appear, covered with a layer of greyish things,
resembling heaps of stones, but which undulate
and give forth a murmur : 'tis an innumerable
and serried crowd, ten thousand people, perhaps, clothed uniformly in long grey robes and
lowered hoods; a mass absolutely compact and
of a single neutral shade, as might be heaps
of stones or bones.   It brings to mind those
primitive crowds, composed of nomad peoples,
to whom it is no matter whether they are here
or elsewhere;   those multitudes who followed
the prophets into the deserts of Judea and
Arabia.

Our arrival is signalled from afar; a movement travels through these masses of human
bodies ; a general murmur of curiosity ascends ;
all the yellowish spots, which stand for faces on
the tops of these heaps of grey wool, are turned
towards us.   Then, in an irresistible impulse of
curiosity, the whole crowd wavers, runs, spreads,
rushes upon our horses and envelops us.

We advance with the utmost difficulty, and
the Arabs of our escort are hard put to it, by
use of thong and stick and musket butt, to clear
a way through the multitude, which breaks
yelling before our passage.   We are now in the
middle of the market; on the ground, at the
feet of this crowd, which ranges itself more or
less in line to make way for us, is a layer of

kneeling camels and sleeping donkeys, which, for their part, do not move. All sorts of absurd-looking commodities are spread out on the ground on odds and ends of mats. There is an infinity of little low tents, beneath which are sold spices, saffron, jujube, pigments for colouring the wool of sheep and the nails of women. There is a sinister-looking shambles marked by an interminable line of wooden gibbets supporting the flayed carcasses of beasts and ill-smelling remnants of every sort—lungs, entrails. Live beasts, too, are on sale, by auction—horses, bullocks and slaves; on every side we hear the little bells of the water-sellers, who carry their merchandise on their back in hairy leathern bottles and offer it to each and all in one same glass for a *flouc* (a seventh of a halfpenny). And some old women, almost naked, carry about long sticks bearing at the end those white rags, which, in Morocco, are the ensign of the mendicant poor.

The kaids responsible for our heads recommend us to march in a solid group, without separating from one another by so much as the length of a horse. They have their reasons for that, no doubt; but nevertheless the curiosity around us does not seem malevolent. Indeed, when the first tumult has died down, and some of the women begin to intone in our honour the

F

strident: " You ! You ! You ! " of festival,
the cry is taken up by the whole crowd, spreading, like a train of powder, into the distances of
the market.

" You ! You ! You ! " As we depart, the
whole grey assemblage gives out a multitudinous
sound, shrill and persistent, but becoming
fainter in the distance, until it resembles the
sound the grasshoppers make in their hours
of high exaltation under the July sun.

Soon the thousands of burnouses and human
heads disappear behind the undulations of the
rolling, sandy plain. The solitudes resume
their sway.

The country becomes increasingly flat. The
high mountains, amid which we travelled during
the first few days, are disappearing behind us,
and the horizon in front of us is becoming
more monotonous.

But there is no end to the wonderful fantasias
which pass like a tempest on the flank of our
column, with savage cries and fusillades, with
waving burnouses and streaming manes. We
scarcely take any notice of them now, except
to keep out of the way when we hear them
coming. Nevertheless, they are more astonishing than ever; mingled with them now are
feats of daring acrobatism; there are men
standing upright on their saddles, others on

their heads, their legs in the air, and they pass, thus, with the swiftness of lightning, like circus clowns practising in open country ; two horsemen hurl themselves upon each other at an unbridled gallop and, as they pass, contrive, without overthrow or slackening, to exchange their muskets, and to give each other a kiss. An old white-bearded chief points with pride to a group of twelve horsemen charging in line —superb all of them. They are his twelve sons. He desires the Minister's attention drawn to them and that everyone should know.

.   .   .   .

A river which we cross by a ford marks the boundary of the territory of the Sefiann.

We enter the territory of the Beni-Malek, whose kaid awaits us on the farther bank with two hundred horsemen. He is the Kaid Abassi, a favourite of the Sultan, an old man with an extremely shrewd and intelligent face, whose daughter, we are told, married at Fez the Grand Vizier, amid great rejoicings. We have arranged to halt in his territory, for the sake of his *mouna*, which is renowned throughout Morocco.

The country grows flatter and flatter and the mountains have almost disappeared. Everywhere sand and daffodils. Gradually the horizon becomes an immense straight line, unbroken as the line of the sea, and seems vaster than ever.

At about midday we make a halt, for our midday meal, at the village of the kaid. It is like all other Moroccan villages. The cottages, of dried earth, are low and covered with reeds, and surrounded by a thorny hedge of bluish cacti; storks have built nests on all the roofs, and grasshoppers chirp everywhere in the neighbourhood.

After we have had luncheon in our tent encumbered with monstrous pyramids of cous-cous, we are invited to take tea with the kaid.

His house is the only one in the surrounding country that is built of masonry. It is sur-rounded like a citadel by a series of little ramparts of great antiquity, made of bricks faced with a yellow glaze. In addition, formid-able hedges of cacti render it almost inaccessible. It opens by three whitewashed Moorish arcades on to an interior garden full of orange-trees.

The orange-trees are in blossom and the garden is fragrant with an exquisite perfume; it is melancholy, nevertheless, invaded as it is by weeds, with its general air of neglect, and confined thus within these old walls, while all around the space is so vast, so free, so open, It suggests at once a prison-yard and the nest of a vulture.

We are received in an apartment that opens on to this mournful garden. Within, there is scarcely anything : whitewash on the walls; and on the floor, carpets and cushions. The floor itself is of mosaics, with a deep hole dug in the earth to receive the dregs of the tea-cups, the superfluity of the hot water of the samovars. And in the wall at the back are other holes, like loopholes, through which the eyes of the imprisoned women watch us drink.

.   .   .   .

We mount our horses again at about two o'clock, to continue our march to the Sebu, one of the largest rivers of Morocco, and indeed of Western Africa, which we are to cross this evening.

In front of us, on the plain, a group of men, looking like ancient suppliants, are leading a little ox by the horns. At the moment the Minister passes comes the flash of an un-sheathed sabre ; two deft blows and it is done : the two hamstrings of the ox are severed, and it sinks in a pool of blood, turning pitifully upon us eyes full of anguish. How featly might these fellows lop off a head ! The sacrifice accomplished, the suppliants hand to the Minister their written request : it is a long and ancient history, going back I know not how many years, in which are recorded the rivalries

of families, assassinations, inexplicable things.
It will go to swell the multitude of complicated
matters that have to be adjusted at Fez, with
the Grand Vizier.

.   .   .   .

We do not see the Sebu until we are close upon
it.   It is a river as large as the Seine at Rouen,
which rolls its muddy waters in a very deep
bed between banks of greyish earth.   It serpentines in the plain, which is boundless as the
sea.

Our camp, which continued on its way during
our midday halt, is already pitched on the
opposite bank.   We cross in two boats, in
many turns, amid great uproar.   Some caravans
which have been held up for some two hours by
the passage of our tents and baggage encumber
the vicinity ; for the moment the place is very
animated, very lively.

The river Sebu makes a sharp line of de-
marcation between hither and farther Morocco.
As soon as it is crossed one gets an impression
of more complete separation from the contemporary world, of more complete absorption
in the sombre land of Al Moghreb.   We are
still within the territory of the Beni-Malek,
but very close to that of the Beni-Hassem—a
dangerous and marauding tribe.   It is, moreover, a maxim well known to travellers in

Morocco that, when once the Sebu is crossed, it behoves one to be circumspect, and keep good guard.

On this farther bank the nature of the soil and of the plants is completely changed. Instead of sand and daffodils we have now, to our great surprise, a dark, rich earth, like that of the plains of Normandy, covered with a thick, abundant growth of colza, marigolds and mallows, into which we sink to the knees.

It is the hour of sunset. The light is clear and cold. It might be a seascape, so straight are the unbroken lines of the horizon. Indeed, a tranquil sea is not more level than this wild plain, which extends for a good forty miles. On one side only, above the desert of herbage, a chain of very distant mountains appears like a little festoon of crude and frozen blue. The distances are absolutely yellow with flowers, a golden-yellow, while the sky above, cloudless, infinitely empty, is of a greenish-yellow, very pale.

The always cold wind of the night rises on this steppe of mallows and marigolds; it sets us shivering after the burning sun of the day; it brings a melancholy of winter to this place, where nowhere around could we find a hearth to shelter us.

It is the most disagreeable encampment we

have had since our departure. Under our
tents, marigolds and mallows form a high,
thick mass, which is irritating, discomforting ;
it is as if we were lying in the middle of a
flower bed. Vainly we trample them underfoot ;
they make a pretence of being crushed, giving
out an acrid odour, but recover obstinately,
rise up and make the carpets and mats billow.
They fill the air with an excessive moisture.
And from them, too, as crowning discomfort,
issue grasshoppers, crickets, mantes, slugs,
which all night long wander over us.

CHAPTER XIV

11th April.

A NIGHT of heavy dew. Water trickles everywhere under my tent, which is filled with a thick mist and the accentuated, bitter odour of marigolds.

Until daybreak the watchers sang around the camp, in conflict with sleep. In the grey dawn their voices gave place to those of the quails, calling in the herbage.

We strike camp at six o'clock and are in the saddle at seven.

First, we proceed across the immense plain, escorted by our friends of yesterday, the Beni-Malek, to the number of two hundred. The air seems warmer on this southern bank of the river, and the country more inhospitable than ever.

Over the infinite yellow of the colza and marigolds stretches a dark, stormy sky, showing patches of deep blue.

Then come regions all white, mile after mile of camomile flowers, which we crush in passing. Their perfume impregnates our horses for the rest of the day.

After travelling for two hours we encounter the horsemen of the Beni-Hassem, who are awaiting us.

Brigands, in very truth; their aspect leaves no room for doubt of it.

But superb brigands; the most handsome faces of bronze that I have ever seen, the most graceful poses, the shapeliest muscular arms, the most beautiful horses. Long curls of hair, escaping from their turbans above the ears, contribute to give a strangely disquieting effect to their physiognomies.

Their chief advances, smiling very graciously, and offers his hand to the Minister. We shall be in absolute security in his territory, of that there is no shadow of a doubt; from the moment we become his guests he is answerable to the Sultan for our heads with his own. It is always much better, in fact, to be entrusted to his guard than merely to camp in his vicinity; that is an axiom well known in Morocco.

He is a remarkable type of the bandit, this chief of the Beni-Hassem. His beard, his hair, his eyebrows, white as snow, show up very clearly against the mummy-yellow of the rest of his face; his aquiline profile has a supreme distinction. He rides a white horse covered with a silken cloth of peach-blossom pink, with bridle and harness of rose-coloured silk,

high-peaked saddle of rose-coloured velvet, and
large stirrups inlaid with gold. He is robed all
in white, like a saint, in waves of transparent
muslin. When he extends his arm to shake
hands, his gesture discloses a wonderful double
pagoda sleeve, first that of his shirt of white silk
gauze, then that of his under-robe, also of silk,
and of an old sea-green altogether exquisite.
In truth, you might imagine that you saw the
tapering fingers and antique cuffs of some
dowager marquise issuing from the burnous
of this old robber.

We perceive in the distance the reserve of his
horsemen, the most handsome and most richly
caparisoned, whom, in the cunning of his stage-
craft, he had left behind, so that they might
surge like a hurricane from the background
of the plain. They bear down upon us at full
speed, with ferocious cries, admirable thus,
seen in front, through the smoke of their
fusillade, in their frenzy of noise and swiftness.
Unrolled turbans stream, harnesses break,
muskets explode. And the earth is torn up
by the hoofs of their horses, so that we see
black particles like grape-shot flying on all
sides.

Needs must they rob travellers, indeed, to
be able to show such magnificence ! All the
bridles and all the harnesses are of silk, matching

marvellously the covering of the horse and the costume of its rider : blue, pink, water-green, salmon, amaranth, jonquil. All the stirrups are inlaid with gold. All the horses have, as breastpiece, a kind of long valance of velvet magnificently embroidered with gold and held in place by large clasps of carved silver, or of precious stones. How mean now seem the poor fantasias of the first days, in the neighbourhood of Tangier, which had seemed to us so striking.

The luncheon, too, with this old chief, is savage, like his territory, like his tribe. On the ground, on the carpet of yellow flowers, at a chance spot in the midst of the boundless plain, he offers us a black couscous, with sheep roasted whole, served on large wooden platters. And while we are tearing, with our fingers, fragments of flesh from these huge joints, come suppliants again to sacrifice before our Minister a ram, which ensanguines the grass around us.

.   .   .   .

Throughout the afternoon the plain unrolls as level and monotonous as ever ; but towards evening it becomes more arid, more African, and mint and thorny jujube-trees replace the colza and marigolds. From the sky, quite bereft of cloud, falls a hot and mournful light. From distance to distance, a carcass of a horse or of a camel marks the beaten track. And in the infrequent little villages of grey thatch, lost amid the desert-like expanses, we begin to see the round conical hut, the Soudanese hut, the hut of Senegal.

We change tribes at about four o'clock, having had to traverse but a very narrow corner of the territory of the Beni-Hassem. We enter now the territory of the Sherarbas, who are an inoffensive people entirely in the hands of the Sultan. But our safety amongst them is doubtful, on account of their dangerous neighbours, who will no longer be responsible for us.

At about six o'clock we camp at a point where the roads to Fez and Mequinez divide, near the venerable tomb of Sidi-Gueddar, who was a great Moroccan saint.

This tomb, like all the marabouts of Algeria and all the *koubas* of Morocco, is a small square building surmounted by a round dome. It is riven, cracked by the sun, extremely old. A white flag floats beside it, on the end of a stick, to indicate to passing caravans that it is meritorious to place offerings there ; a mat, held down by heavy stones, is spread on the ground to receive them, and the pieces of money thrown there by pious travellers are left to the custody of the birds of the air, until the priests come to collect them.

With all politeness we are recommended not to approach too close to this tomb of Sidi-Gueddar; so holy is it that the presence of us Christians there would be a sacrilege.

.   .   .   .

The mountains which, this morning, barely showed their little blue festoons on the very limit of the flat horizon are now no more than five or six miles from us; all day long they have been mounting into the sky, and to-morrow we shall cross them. This evening we are in a region of lucerne, flowering with that excess which is characteristic of Moroccan plants. In our neighbourhood are some villages of thatch; as the twilight gathers we can hear the barking of dogs, just as in our own country-side, and little hooded shepherds bring in their droves of bleating sheep and goats; over all is an air of pastoral innocence, of reassuring security. The road to Fez, moreover, passes quite close to our camp, so close in fact that the ropes of our tents cross it, and the caravans, which continue to pass till nightfall, have to make a detour in the lucerne, for fear of entangling the feet of their camels. And this track is so beaten here, and the plain besides is so perfectly level, that it might be a real highway, easy to walk along, tempting for a stroll. One must have lived some time in

Morocco, where walking is everywhere difficult, and often impossible, to understand the seduction of a proper road, the desire which seizes us for a good honest tramp on so fair a night as this.

We must deny ourselves, however, to-night more than ever. Strict orders have been given not to leave the camp. Not only have we the Beni-Hassem for neighbours, but, and this more especially, we are not more than an hour's journey from the mountains where dwell the terrible Zemur, inexorable fanatics, robbers, murderers, and for many years in open rebellion against the government of Fez. The Sultan himself, when he travels with his camp of thirty thousand men, avoids this country of the Zemur.

In the first rays of the moon, after the grave, ritual arrival of the *mouna*, the guards around the camp are doubled, all muskets loaded, with orders to allow no one to approach and to sing till morning, beating their drums to keep themselves in watchfulness. The kaid responsible seems nervous, restless and does not lie down.

CHAPTER XV

12th April.

THROUGHOUT the night they have sung and beaten their drums, and this morning, under a sky darkened with clouds, we are awakened, and none of us has been murdered. What is more, as we are getting up, a kind of complementary *mouna* is brought to us, consisting of new milk in amphoræ and some excellent butter.

We have before us to-day a march of five and twenty miles, and hardly are we embarked upon it than a fine cold rain begins to fall. Another hour and a half yet of plain, through fields of colza and barley, through fields of lucerne, where innumerable flocks of sheep are grazing. Under this cloudy sky we might again imagine that we were in some luxuriant Normandy, were it not for the pointed huts of the villages and the burnouses of the shepherds. The fantasias, which are continued in our honour, are much less wonderful than those of the Beni-Hassem ; we feel that these good Sherarbas are far less warlike and far less rich ; and then, somehow, one gets tired of it all, it becomes a fatigue, at length, to be thus obliged at every moment, with the rain driving into your eyes, to get out of the way of these horsemen, who come upon you like the wind, firing their muskets in your ears and frightening the horses.

Leaving on our right the dangerous country of the Zemur, we become involved in the mountains, which we have to cross before the close of day. The ascent is laborious, under a torrential rain, through a succession of narrow, bounded gorges sown with wheat and barley. Following the custom in Morocco, we trample all these growths underfoot; there will remain far more than can ever be harvested. Up the slopes, often very steep, we struggle through a clayey mire, soaked and sticky, which accumulates about the feet of our horses in enormous pads; at every step we feel ourselves slipping; our laden mules fall one after another, rolling over with our tents, our mattresses, our baggage, in quagmires of mud, in improvised torrents formed on every side by the diluvian rain.

The kaid of the Sherarbas and his horsemen left us at the boundary of their territory, and the chief of the region in which we now are has not come to meet us, which is an extraordinary circumstance. For the first time we are without escort, alone.

G

With our fallen mules, with our men bemired in the clayey mud, our straggling column is now more than two miles long. And what are we to do? Where are we to stop? Where to put up? Where to find a shelter of any sort in this country without houses, without trees, with not so much as a hut where we might seek a refuge?

In this plight we meet a column at least as numerous as our own; first a number of horsemen, and behind them a train of camels carrying a quantity of veiled women and baggage. It is, it appears, the caravan of a kaid of a distant province who is returning from a visit to the Sultan. These people, like us, are in difficulties in the clayey and slippery mud.

At last our dilatory chief arrives with his troop. He is full of excuses; he was in pursuit of three Zemur brigands very dreaded in the country; he has succeeded in capturing them, with their horses. They are now confined in safe custody in his house, whence they will be taken to Fez to undergo the "punishment of salt," as ordained by law.

And whilst we continue to climb very laboriously in the rain, with slippings and downfallings, through these horrible little valleys which are all alike, with walls of greyish earth, I have described to me in detail this "punishment of salt," which is of very ancient tradition.

The Sultan's barber, it appears, is charged with it. The culprit, tightly bound, is brought to some public place, preferably to the market-place. With a razor, lengthwise in the palm of each hand, four slits are cut to the bone. By stretching the palm, the lips of these four bleeding cuts are made to gape as much as possible and are filled with salt. The hands thus slashed are then closed, the tips of the fingers being inserted into the several slits, and in order that this atrocious arrangement may last till death, the hand is enclosed in a kind of tight glove, made of wet ox-hide, which shrinks as it dries. The cutting finished, the culprit is taken back to his cell, where, in exceptional cases, he is fed, in order to prolong his agony. From the first moment, in addition to the indescribable suffering, he has the anguish of knowing that this horrible glove will never be removed, that his fingers embedded in the quivering wounds will never be released, that no one in the world will take pity on him, that neither day nor night will bring a respite to his writhings and his shrieks of suffering. But the worst, so I am told, does not come till some days later—when the nails, growing into the hand, dig ever deeper into the cloven flesh.

Then the end is near; some die of tetanus, others are driven to dash their head against the wall.

I beseech at once those persons with humanitarian notions conceived in the comfort of their easy-chairs not to cry out against the cruelty of the Moroccans. In the first place, I would bid them remember that here, in Al Moghreb, we are still in the Middle Ages, and goodness knows our Europe of the Middle Ages did not lack inventive imagination in the matter of punishments. Then, again, the Moroccans, like all men who remain primitive, are far from having our nervous sensibility; and as, moreover, they hold death in absolute contempt, our simple guillotine would seem in their eyes a chastisement so unmeaning as to deter no one. In a country where journeys are so long and the routes absolutely unguarded, one cannot blame this people for having introduced into their code something which causes the brigands of the mountains a little reflection.

. . . .

By steady climbing we reach the summits of the chain, and, in a fair interval between two showers, behold the plain beyond outspread beneath us. It is much smaller than that of the Sebu, but wonderfully fertile and well cultivated : a kind of inner circus bounded beyond by mountains, amongst which we shall have to camp to-morrow night, and which are far higher than those we have just ascended.

Half-way down the slope which we are now about to descend is perched a village : a hundred or so huts of thatch, with enclosures of cactus, grouped around an old Moorish building, which is at once the citadel and the residence of the kaid. The country is still almost destitute of trees ; no more than the olives and orange-trees of a mysterious garden enclosed within the walls of the little fortress.

We see the village, naturally, from above, in a bird's-eye view ; and thus the terrace on the top of the chief's house has the appearance of a public square with veiled women, in white and rose-coloured robes, strolling about, their faces upturned to watch us coming.

After a rapid and dangerous descent over scattered boulders, we halt for the night near the walls of the garden, on a kind of common camping ground used by passing caravans. The long coarse grass is trodden, dirty, infested with vermin, littered with the debris of fowls and couscous, and marked with large black circles made by the fires of the nomads. Never before have we camped at a spot sullied in this manner.

The men of our escort mow the filthy grass

with their long sabres, less used to this business,
no doubt, than to the lopping off of heads.
One after another, and long after us, come our
wet tents, which are set up with great difficulty
in a gale of wind.   At an improvised session,
the muleteers are bastinadoed for their luckless
management of the beasts.   Last of all arrive
our provisions, on poor little mules that have
fallen a score of times and are raw and bleeding
at the knees ; and at about three o'clock in the
afternoon, faint with hunger, we make our
luncheon on cold, rain-sodden fare.   All the
children of the village, all the comical little
burnouses, all the priceless little hoods, come
gambolling about our camp, calling down upon
us all kinds of maledictions, mocking us with
all kinds of insults.   We ask for some wood in
order that we may dry ourselves a little, but
there is none to be had in the district, which
is completely destitute even of shrubs ; they
bring us bundles of dry thistles and some ine
branches which give out large flames and a
great quantity of smoke, but very little heat.

Camped half-way down the mountain,
separated by a hedge of aloes from a fearful
sheer descent into the plain below, we see at our
feet the interminable road to Fez, continuing
without intermission, through new barley-
fields, through new prairies, until it is lost in

the heights of the distant mountains beyond. It is more and more clearly marked by the constant tramping of the caravans; it has more and more the appearance of a real road; and it becomes more animated also in proportion as we draw nearer to the holy city. Between the showers, in the extreme transparency of the atmosphere, we perceive below, as from the height of an observatory, long processions of horsemen, of burnoused pedestrians, of camels and asses laden with merchandise; all this microscopically · small, like a ceaseless promenade of marionettes at the bottom of a vast empty void. For Fez is not only the religious capital of the Occident, the most holy, after Mecca, of the towns of Islam, whither priests come to study from all points of Africa; it is also the commercial centre of the West, communicating by the ports of the north with Europe, and by way of Tafilet and the desert with the black Soudan as far as Timbuctoo and Senegambia.

And all this activity has nothing in common with ours, is expended, as it was a thousand years ago, in ways that are quite other than our ways, by routes that to us are utterly unknown.

CHAPTER XVI

13th April.

IT has rained in torrents through the night, and the wind has almost carried away our tents. Rising from damp beds, we put on wet clothing and boots full of water, and get under way again beneath a sky uniformly covered with a kind of grey crape.

After crossing this new plain we become involved in the defiles of these new mountains. The thought that we shall have to repeat this journey in the opposite direction, before we can leave this sombre land, oppresses us a little at times. But we are sustained by the hope that to-morrow evening we shall be within sight of the holy city—like those crusaders and pilgrims of old, to whom it was promised, after many days and nights of marching, that they were about to behold at last the Mecca or Jerusalem of their dreams.

Towards midday, in the mountains, the sky clears little by little, but very quickly, till finally it is swept free from cloud; the first rays of the sun come to warm us again; then the true light of Africa returns, splendid,

incomparable; in an hour the transformation is
complete, the earth is dry, the sky wholly blue,
the air burning. And how everything changes
its appearance in the radiant sunshine! We are
travelling now through a succession of delicious
valleys, the sandy soil of which is carpeted
with grass and flowers. Especially noticeable
are the giant fennels, their flowering stems
resembling yellow trees, which are garlanded
with the large pink blossoms of a bindweed
similar to that of our gardens. Yellow and rose
—those are the two prevailing colours in the zone
of Eden through which we are passing to-day.
The mountains begin to be wooded with dark
olive-trees, and their basalt crests, rising bare
out of the verdure, resemble the pipes of an
organ; and, above these nearer summits, in
the wonderfully clear air, we can perceive
others, more distant and higher, prodigiously
high indeed; and those are of lapis blue.

Not a village, not a house, not a sign of
cultivation; nothing but flowers again, and a
country astonishingly perfumed.

But we meet continually numbers of men
and beasts; bands of wayfarers, almost nude,
carrying their clothes folded on their heads;
fair women astraddle on mules, so closely
veiled, even when travelling, that we can only
divine their large black eyes; flocks of sheep

and flocks of goats; and camels above all, slow and grave, carrying to Fez, with a swaying motion like the rolling of a ship, enormous bales.

From time to time we cross a swiftly running stream; a solitary palm-tree grows usually on the bank.

At each of the fords are old men squatting before heaps of oranges; for a sou, you may take as many as you please, within reason.

Towards evening we reach the Oued M'Kez, a rapidly flowing river, across which—marvellous to tell—is thrown a bridge—a bridge of narrow, rounded arches, decorated with green tiles.

The central pillar is marked with the mysterious seal of Solomon: two interlaced triangles — and, on either side, pictures in mosaic framed with green tell, in entwined letters, who was the architect of the bridge and what praises the travellers who use it owe to the God of Islam. Time and sun have endued the masonry with a rare, warm, almost roseate hue, which harmonises marvellously with the faded green of the bordering faience. And the scene, too, is tranquil, pastoral, imprinted with the melancholy of abandon and bygone time.

We have marched throughout the fresh overcast morning, throughout the burning hours of midday, and now it is the magical and golden hour of sunset. We have reached the territory of the Zerhanas, who are husbandmen and shepherds of the mountains, and on the other side of this bridge, in a plain of red anemones, surrounded by wooded summits, we are going to camp amongst them.

Our little nomad town is already there, outspread on the ground, on the fragrant herbage, in the dying rays of the sun.

One after another the poles of our tents are upraised, topped with their sconces of gleaming copper; then the large closed umbrellas open, showing their rows of black arabesques; the tightened cords stretch them, straighten them, fix them; the hanging draperies are added, and the thing is done: our houses are built, our camp is pitched whole and entire, glad to dry itself in the good warm air.

And how gay and charming it is, this French camp of ours, in the activity of arrival, at this softly luminous hour of evening, with its whiteness in this green country, with the striking colours contributed by the caftans of our Arabs, with all the high-peaked saddles of red cloth and all the multi-coloured trappings scattered about the prairie of anemones. Around there is an animation which seems to be the simple life of ancient days: fantasias galloping past at full speed; flocks brought by half-nude shepherds to drink at the river; the Sultan's boat appearing in the distance on the shoulders of its forty white-robed bearers; the *mouna* making its entry (a little ox and twelve sheep led by the horns); then a messenger from the Grand Vizier, who has come from Fez to meet us, bringing to the Minister a greeting of welcome.

And over all this the wonderful golden light begins to fade; the sun, which is about to disappear behind the high summits, lengthens disproportionately the shadows of the horsemen, the strange shadows of the motionless camels; it illumines only the extreme points of our tents—only their copper sconces, which gleam still; then it is extinguished and we are plunged at once into a blue twilight.

. . . .

In the moonlight our little French camp is even more entrancing. It is one of those African nights, gentle, calm, radiant, luminous, such as are never seen in our countries of the north; after the cold and the obstinate rain, it is with a sense almost of intoxication that one experiences again all this that one had forgotten. The bright full moon rides high in a clear star-strewn heaven. Our white tents, spotted with black arabesques, have an air

of mystery, arranged thus in circle under the
blue light that falls from above; their metal
sconces still gleam confusedly; here and there
little red fires are burning in the grass, little
flames are dancing; around, white-robed men
are squatting in groups on mats; and from
these groups, ere they fall asleep, comes the
mournful sound of guitars. Curlews are calling
in the outer silence, in the sonority of the night.
The neighbouring mountains seem to have
drawn closer to us, so clearly can we see their
recesses, their boulders, their suspended woods.
The air is filled with suave, exotic perfumes,
and over all broods a serene tranquillity which
defies expression.

Oh! the joyous life of the open air, the free
life of the road! What a pity that to-morrow
need ever come! What a pity that our
journey must have its end!

CHAPTER XVII

14th April.

OF this country of the Zerhanas I shall always remember the fresh hours of the morning passed on the bank of the Oued M'Kez, amid that enchanting scenery, on that carpet of red anemones. Near our encampment a little wood of venerable olive-trees sheltered some shepherds and their goats. In the surrounding mountains, among the boulders and brushwood, were two or three hamlets, perched like eagles' eyries. Nothing African in the landscape, apart from the excess and splendour of the light; and even our countrysides sometimes attain this brilliance of verdure, this clearness of blue sky, on certain privileged days of the beautiful month of June. So much so that the illusion took hold of us completely that we were in some wild corner of France; and to see on the pathways, amid the tall, flowering herbage, the frenzied fantasias, the Bedouins and the camels, seemed even passing strange.

CHAPTER XVIII

On horseback again at eight o'clock, we become involved in the mountains which straightway change their appearance, becoming very African now, rugged, ravined, with ardent tones of yellow ochre, and golden-brown, and reddish-brown. Broad stretches of moorland unroll slowly, carpeted with thorny jujube-trees and scanty bushes. At wide intervals, in the background of expanses devoured by light, we perceive the *douars* of nomad Bedouins, rings of brown tents, with cattle in the middle; on solitary heights scorched by the overpowering sun, they make perfect little circles, and in the distance look like very dark brown stains. And the superheated air quivers everywhere, rippling like a pool when its surface is ruffled by a light breeze.

.　　.　　.　　.　　.　　.　　.

After the midday halt we pass through a cultivated valley: fields of barley of an emerald-green glistening in the sunshine and pinked with red poppies.

Since morning we have seen nothing but solitudes, and we look about for the habitations of the people who have sown this ground.

At last in a recess we discover their village, which seems half fantastical; three tall black rocks, pointed like Gothic spires, stand upright side by side, looking strangely out of place in the midst of this prairie of green velvet; each of them is crowned by a stork's nest; a wall of beaten earth surrounds them at their base, all three together, and at different heights on their sides hang a dozen Lilliputian houses.

There seems to be no one about this singular village, which is guarded only by the three storks, motionless on the summits of the three rocks; all around, nothing but silence and the prostration of a summer noon.

. . . .

And, at last, at last, at about four o'clock in the afternoon, the immense emptiness opens once more before us. A new sea of uninterrupted herbage, a green and yellow sea of barley and flowering fennel—the plain of Fez! Far away, the great Atlas makes for it an imposing girdle of white, glistening, snow-capped crests. Five more miles through the plain and suddenly, appearing from behind the slope of a mountain which recedes like the side-piece of a stage setting, the holy city is slowly revealed to us.

At first it is only a white line, white as the snow of the Atlas, which is distorted and confused, like a thing insubstantial, by the continuous mirage : the aqueducts, we are told, the great whitened aqueducts that carry water to the gardens of the Sultan.

Then this same mountain slope, steadily with-drawing, begins to disclose to us high grey ramparts, surmounted by high grey towers. And it comes to us as a surprise to see Fez so sombre in colour amid a plain so green; we had imagined it white in the midst of sand. It has an air of unutterable sadness, it is true; but, seen from afar off, surrounded by these verdant growths, it is difficult to believe that before us lies the impenetrable holy city, and our expectation of it is almost disappointed. Slowly, however, we become impressed by the surrounding calm; we begin to feel that a strange sleep broods over this town, which is so high, so large, which, in its approaches, has no railway, nor any carriage, nor any road; nothing but these grassy tracks along which pass, slowly, the silent caravans.

We camp, for the last time, at a place called Ansala-Faradji, half-an-hour away from the embattled walls.

We shall enter pompously to-morrow morn-ing : all the musicians, all the troops, the whole population, including even the women, have received orders to come in mass to meet us.

H

CHAPTER XIX

15th April.

ONCE more we awaken under a dark lowering sky, feeling that torrents of water, veritable deluges, are suspended over our heads.

This last morning in camp is more animated than usual. The pompous entry we are about to make necessitates many preparations. Our gala uniforms are withdrawn from the cases, our gold lace, our medals; and the African guards are busied polishing our arms and the harness of our horses.

" The order of the march," elaborated yesterday evening in the Minister's tent, is communicated to us at breakfast; we are to go, be it understood, no longer in confusion, each according to his individual fancy, but in good order, four abreast in four ranks, correctly aligned as for a military " march past."

·   ·   ·   ·   ·   ·   ·

In compliance with a request made to us yesterday evening by direction of the Sultan, we mount our horses at ten o'clock precisely, in order that we may not disturb certain religious Offices of the morning by arriving too early, and in order, also, not to interfere with the midday prayers by arriving too late.

To reach the gates of Fez we have about three-quarters of an hour of slow march, at walking pace or at the gentle trot of parade.

After ten minutes' travelling, the town, of which we have yet seen but a part, appears in its entirety. It is truly very large and very solemn behind its high blackish walls, which exceed in height all the old towers of its mosques. The veil of dark clouds is rent beyond, revealing the snows of the Atlas, to which the stormy sky gives changing colours, sometimes coppery, sometimes livid.

Outside the walls two or three hundred grouped tents make a mass of white things. And the whole plain, all these green fields of barley, are swarmed by little grey dots, which are apparently the hooded heads of human multitudes that have come out to watch our arrival.

These white tents, outside the town, are the camp of the *tholbas* (students), who at this very time are making their annual holiday in the country. But the word "student" is ill suited to describe these sober and grave young men. When I speak of them, I shall continue to use the word *tholba*, which is untranslatable. (It is well known, of course, that Fez contains

the most celebrated of Mussulman universities;
that two or three thousand students come from
all parts of Northern Africa, follow there the
courses of the great mosque of Karaouin, one
of the most sacred sanctuaries of Islam.)
The *tholbas* are on holiday to-day and help
to swell, no doubt, the astonishing crowd that
awaits us.

Never was sky more stormy, more unnatur-
ally black; never was light of day more mournful. The plain over which this sombre vault is
spread is, as it were, walled by high mountains,
the summits of which are lost in the tenebrous
sky. And in front of us, on the limit of the
horizon, the strange old town which is the goal
of our journey outlines its denticulated silhouette, just below the fantastic opening in
which the Atlas shows its glistening snows.
A broad network of little parallel tracks,
traced in the grass by the fantasy of the camel-
drivers, almost simulates a road, and the ground
too is so level that one could march in good
order anywhere one pleased.

We begin to enter amongst the crowd, which
is clothed, as always, in grey wool, grey burnouses and lowered hoods. They watch us
simply, and, in proportion as we pass, turn and
follow us, but the faces remain indifferent, un-
decipherable; it is not possible to distinguish

in them an expression either of sympathy or
dislike. And all the mouths are closed; to-day
there is everywhere that same silence of sleep
which weighs upon this people, upon these
towns, upon this entire country, whenever
there is not a momentary frenzy of movement
and noise.

Here now is the head of a double line of
horsemen, ranked as far as eye can see, to the
gates of the town no doubt, to form for us a
guard of honour. Superb horsemen, in gala
dress, their costumes cunningly harmonised
with the trappings of their horses : on green
saddles, pink caftans ; on yellow saddles, violet
caftans; on orange saddles, blue caftans. And
the transparent woollen muslins, which envelop them in draped folds, conceal these
colours, subdue them to a uniform veiled pale-
ness, making of all these horsemen personages
almost white, whose magnificent under-robes
and brilliant colours appear only fitfully and
for brief moments.

The double alignment forms a kind of imposing avenue, about thirty yards wide, which
is prolonged for a great distance in front of us ;
and we are there alone, separated from the
crowd, which grows continuously on right and
left in the green fields. The heads of these
horsemen and of their horses are turned

towards us; they remain motionless, while,
behind them, the multitude moves solidly,
immensely, in a silence which becomes almost
an obsession; it follows us, in measure as we
pass, as if we drew it after us by some kind of
magnet; and all the time it is becoming denser
and spreading farther and farther into the
plain. As at our entry into Czar, there are
men on foot and men on horseback; others,
three or four together, legs down-hanging, on
an ass or a mule; fathers who have brought
with them their little ones, some on the crupper,
others astraddle on the neck of their beasts.
The ground, trodden and soft, deadens the
sound of all these footsteps, and the mouths
continue to be mute; but the eyes are fixed
upon us. It is a strange variety of silence,
full of muffled trampings, of rustling cloaks,
of innumerable breathings. Now and then a
shower falls for some seconds on our heads, like
a swift and furtive watering, and then stops,
carried away by a gust of wind; the threatening
deluge decides not to fall and the vault remains
as black as ever. Beyond, the walls of Fez
climb higher and higher into the sky, assuming
a formidable aspect that recalls Damietta or
Stamboul.

Amongst these thousands of grey burnouses,
all alike dirty and full of holes, amongst these

thousands of faces obstinately turned upon us,
which follow us behind the screen of cavalry,
I notice a man, his beard already white,
mounted on a lean mule, who is beautiful as a
god, handsome among the handsome, with a
supreme distinction, and two large eyes of fire.
He is own brother to the Sultan, and there
he is, in shabby cloak, pell-mell with the com-
monest of the people. And in Morocco there
is nothing extraordinary in that : the sultans,
on account of the great number of their fathers'
spouses, have a great many brothers and sisters,
whom it is not always possible to endow with
wealth ; and besides, for many of the descendants of the Prophet, the great religious dream
suffices to fill existence and they live poor
willingly, disdaining worldly comforts.

The hedge of white cavaliers draws to an end
and gives place to a line of unbroken red, a
brilliant red, which stands out sharply against
the monotonous grey of the crowd ; it looks
like a long trail of blood, and is prolonged up
to the gate of the town, the monumental ogive
of which, cut in the high ramparts, now comes in
sight. It is the infantry of the Sultan (which
an English ex-colonel who has passed into the
service of Morocco has recently equipped,
alas ! in the fashion of the Indian sepoys).
Poor wretches these, recruited goodness knows

how, negroes for the most part, and ridiculous
in this new costume. Their bare legs issue
like black sticks from the scarlet folds of their
zouave trousers; after the handsome cavaliers
they look pitiful in the extreme, and at close
quarters give the impression of an army of
monkeys; but in their sum they do well;
their long red lines, bordering the grey crowd,
contribute to the enormous picture an addi-
tional strangeness.

Along the imposing avenue, always open
before us, magnificent personages on horseback
come galloping to meet us, augmenting our
troop, which has much ado to preserve its good
order. The Oriental colouring of their costumes
is subdued under long cream-coloured veils,
draped with inimitable grace and majesty.
First, comes the " lieutenant of the introducer
of Ambassadors," clothed all in green, on a
black horse with trappings of golden-yellow
silk; then the old Kaid Belail, the Court buffoon,
robed in delicate rose-colour; his large negro
face, very droll and very sinister, is crowned
by a turban in the form of a pyramid, of an
enormous pear, recalling the towers of the
Kremlin; then other dignitaries arrive, ministers,
viziers. They all carry, slung across the shoulders
and attached by cords and tassels of a wonderful
variety of colours, long scimitars damascened

in gold, the handles of which are formed of a rhinoceros' horn.

We are about to pass now between a double line of musicians ranked in front of the lines of scarlet infantry. They are passing strange of aspect and costume : negro faces, and long robes which fall straight to the ground and give these fellows the appearance of immense old women in dressing-gowns. Their colours are extravagant, with never a veil to temper them, and arranged now as if of purpose to heighten one the other by force of contrast : a violet robe side by side with one of royal blue ; an orange robe between a robe of ecclesiastical purple and a robe of green. Against the neutral background of the surrounding crowds, and amongst these horsemen veiled in muslin, they form the most oddly brilliant group I have ever seen in any country of the world.

They hold instruments of shining brass of a prodigious size. And, as we arrive before them, they blow into these things, into their long trumpets, their serpents, their monstrous trombones ; and from their blowing results all at once a savage cacophony, almost terrifying in effect. For the first minute we know not whether to laugh or not ; but, somehow, it skirts the grotesque without achieving it ; it is so mournful, their music, and the sky is so black the scenery so grand, the place so strange, that we remain thrilled and serious.

And it is the signal, too, for an immense uproar: the charm of the silence is broken. A prodigious tumult of voices arises from all sides, and other musicians respond from different points: the squealing bagpipes, with their notes like the falsetto cry of a jackal, the heavy-sounding tabours and the long, drawling cries: " Hou! Allah send victorious our Sultan, Sidi Mulai-Hassan. Hou!" A sudden frenzy of noise has taken possession of this hooded crowd, which continues to follow us, continues to run after us.

Then the music ceases, the strange clamour dies; the silence suddenly returns, envelops us anew; and once more we hear nothing but the innumerable rustlings of these hurrying, crowding people; nothing but their thousands of footsteps, muffled by the ground.

Here now are the banners, in line on right and left, floating above the heads of the soldiers —banners of regiments, of corporations, of trades, in silk of every colour, with all kinds of strange devices; many are marked with the two interlaced triangles which form the seal of Solomon.

At the side of this human avenue a superb and colossal personage awaits us on horseback, surrounded by a number of other horsemen who constitute his guard of honour. He is the Kaid El-Meshwar, "the introducer of ambassadors." And here there is a moment of hesitation, almost of anxiety; he remains motionless, evidently hoping that the French Minister will stop and make the first step towards him; but the Minister, careful of the dignity of the embassy, pretends to pass proudly on his white horse, without turning his head, as one who has seen nothing. Then the great kaid decides to yield and, spurring his horse, comes to us; there is a shaking of hands, and, the incident ended to our satisfaction, we continue to advance towards the gates.

.   .   .   .

And now we are about to enter. Scarcely more than a hundred yards in front of us rise the immense ramparts, seeming to thrust their ranks of pointed battlements into the sombre clouds of the sky. On each side of the high, wide-open ogive through which we are about to pass, on slopes rising in steps, appear what look like heaped-up layers of pebbles, but are in fact the massed heads of women, veiled, all of them, in thick wool; they stand there, packed to suffocation, motionless, in a silence of death. Others are perched, in little groups, on the summits of the ramparts and look down upon

us vertically from above. The red and green
and yellow banners are wafted in the air, on the
blackish background of the walls. Mounted on
a rock, a visionary " saint," who has thrown
back her veil, is prophesying in a subdued
voice, her eyes wild, her cheeks painted with
vermilion, holding in her hand a bouquet of
orange blossom and marigolds. Through the
great ogive, grey and mournful, appears, some
distance away, another gateway, also immense,
but quite white, quite new, surrounded by
mosaics and arabesques of blue and rose-colour—
like the door of some magic palace, hidden behind
the dilapidation of this formidable outer wall.

And this picture of arrival, this multitude
at the entrance to the town, this display of
banners, all this belongs wholly to the Middle
Ages, has the grandeur of the fifteenth century,
its rudeness and its sombre simplicity.

.   .   .   .

We enter, and are astonished to find empty
spaces and ruins.

Everybody is outside, no doubt, for here we
meet scarcely a soul. And the gateway with
the blue and rose-coloured arabesques, which
looked so fairy-like in the distance, is dis-
appointing on a closer view ; it is immense,
but it is only a vulgar modern imitation of
the ancient splendours. It gives access to the

quarters of the Sultan which occupy almost the
whole of "Fez-Djedid" (New Fez), and the
walls of which, as high and grim as the ramparts
of the town, we now follow. At the foot of
these outer walls of the palace, a heap of dead
beasts, in a kind of sewer, carcasses of horses
and camels, fills the air with an odour of
putrefaction.

We leave behind us all these formidable
seraglio enclosures, old and crumbling, which
point their battlements into the sky and enclose
one another as in an excess of distrust.

Soon we are in the deserted ground that
separates New Fez from "Fez-Bali" (Old Fez),
where we are to reside. Here we walk on large
uneven stones, on the tops of rocks, rounded
and polished by the age-long friction of the
feet of men and the hoofs of beasts. We make
our way amid quagmires, caverns, cemeteries
as old as Islam, stony hillocks covered with
cacti and aloes, *koubas* (mortuary chapels to
the memory of " saints ") crowned with domes
and ornamented with inscriptions in mosaics of
black faience.

On the crest of a tall rock stands one of these
koubas, very high and as large, almost, as a
mosque ; its old walls are crowned by a line of
women, like birds perched on a ruin, who watch
us through the slits in their veils; all their

painted eyes are bent upon us; above them, on the point of the dome, a large motionless stork, also watching us, completes the extraordinary scaffolding. And behind the *kouba* rise two palm-trees, quite stiff and straight, like plants of metal; their bouquets of yellowed plumes, at the end of interminable stems, stand out sharply against the unchanging blackness of the sky.

At the moment we pass, a rapid and, as it might seem, furious, "You! You! You! You!" descends in our honour from this *kouba*, the women removing the veils from their mouths in order that they may be better heard. And as we raise our heads to look at them, our horses suddenly rear—we thought, at first, at some dead beast lying in the road. But no: before our feet, in the middle of the road, is a gaping hole, large enough to swallow us, flush with the ground, without any sort of protection, which gives access, like an open keystone, to one of those immense subterranean places called "silos," which are dug in Morocco to hide wheat and barley in case of war or famine.

Then I understand the Moroccan expression "to fall into a silo," which means to let oneself be caught in a trap from which it is impossible to escape.

Old Fez is before us : the same intimidating walls, cracked from top to base ; the same gap-toothed battlements. A triple ogival gateway, broad, deep and distorted, exactly similar in design to that of the fortress of the Alhambra, gives us access to the infinitely old and infinitely holy town.

First, a long sinister street, between high, cracked and blackish walls which are unrelieved by any window : only, at wide intervals, barred holes through which curious eyes gaze upon us; then a corner of the covered bazaar, a savage sort of bazaar, savouring already of the black Soudan; and then, suddenly, we plunge into a neighbourhood of gardens.

There, under another form, we find the same air of mournfulness. In single file, now, we pass through a labyrinth of little passages, which turn perpetually upon themselves, and are so narrow that, as we pass, our knees are constantly grazing the walls on either side. Ancient low little walls of clay, cracked by the sun and embellished with yellow lichen, above which rise palm-trees and charming branches of orange-trees in blossom. The red soldiers, who nevertheless are assiduous in their escort, are trampled upon and crushed by our horses, which splash through a black, sticky mud similar to that at Czar-el-Kebir. And in this

maze of passages openings appear only at wide
intervals, and they are small and locked and
barred. It is not very easy to see how one
can enter these mysterious gardens, nor how
one can get out of them.

At length our guide stops us before the oldest
of the doors, the lowest and most narrow,
pierced in the oldest of the walls; it might be
the entrance to a den of thieves, and of very
poverty-stricken thieves at that; but it is
here, nevertheless, that the Ambassador and
his suite are to be lodged!

(I must really apologise for the so-frequent
use of the word " old." But just as, in writing
of Japan, the word " little," I remember,
recurred in spite of me at every line, so here it
is old age, old age tottering and dead, which is
the prevailing impression caused by surrounding
things; it is necessary, once for all, to understand that that of which I speak is all marked
by the usury of the centuries, that the walls
are defaced and corroded by lichen, that the
houses are leaning and crumbling, that all the
angles of the stones are smoothed.)

The passage is so narrow that we experience
some difficulty in dismounting. There is no
time to lose, however. As soon as we get out
of the saddle we have to plunge at once into
the old, low little doorway, in order not to be

crushed by the next horseman who follows
hard upon us, pushed in turn by all the others
in line. One almost falls, in this way, on to
the bayonet of a guard of soldiers commanded
by a kind of janissary, old and black, who will
have orders not to allow any of his new French
guests to go out without an armed escort.

Such an entrance is scarcely cheerful; but,
in Morocco, there is no need to worry about
the exterior of habitations; the most miserable
approaches lead sometimes to palaces of fairies.

The guard passed, we reach a delightful
garden. Large orange-trees covered with white
blossom are planted there in quincunxes,
above a medley of rose-trees, jasmines, garden-
mints and gillyflowers. Then a paved cause-
way leads us to another door, also very low,
at the foot of a high wall, which opens on to a
court of Alhambra, with festooned arcades and
arabesques and mosaics, and fountains playing
in marble basins. It is here that the embassy is to undergo the preliminary three
days of quarantine and " purification " always
imposed on foreigners who are privileged to
enter Fez.

. . . .

In the confusion of arrival I seek out the
Minister to make my request to be allowed
to live alone, elsewhere, in a dwelling that a

providential friend has been good enough to place at my disposal.

The Minister smiles ; he suspects, perhaps, an intention to escape the " purification " and to make forbidden excursions to-morrow. But he consents graciously. And I remount my horse, in the fine, steady rain which now is falling, and go in search of my own private dwelling.

CHAPTER XX

THIS same day of arrival, at nine or ten o'clock in the evening, in the solitude of my house.

Of all the lodgings that have sheltered me during the course of my life, none has ever been more sinister than this, none less commonplace of access. And never has come more suddenly or more completely the impression of strangeness in a strange land, of translation from myself into another personage of a different world and of an anterior epoch.

Around me is the darksome holy city, on which has just descended a cold night, thick with a wintry rain. At sunset Fez closed the gates of its long, crenellated ramparts; then all its interior gates, dividing it into an infinity of wards which, at night-time, do not communicate with one another.

And I dwell in one of these quarters of Fez-Bali (Old Fez), so called in contradistinction to Fez-Djedid (New Fez); and New Fez has been a nest of owls for the last six or eight hundred years.

This Fez-Bali is a labyrinth of dark and hidden streets, which wind in all directions between high blackish walls. And in all the height of these inaccessible houses there are scarcely ever any windows; merely little holes, and even they are carefully barred. The doors, sunk in deep embrasures, are so low that one has to double in two to enter; and they are overlaid in every case with iron, and have enormous nails and spikes and bolts and locks and heavy knockers worn with long use; and all this is warped and wry and rusty—writ with the fantasy of a thousand years.

Of all these little intersecting streets, the narrowest, I think, and the darkest, is mine. One enters it by a low ogive, to find there the darkness almost of night in high noon; it is strewn with refuse, with dead mice, dead dogs; the ground is channelled in the middle in the form of a stream, and one sinks to above the ankles in liquid mud. It has a width of one yard, neither more nor less; when two people meet, hooded always or veiled in white wool like phantoms, they are obliged to flatten themselves against the walls; and when I pass on horseback, anyone coming in the opposite direction is forced to retire or take refuge in one of the doorways, for my stirrups, on right and left, scrape against the houses. Above, the way is narrower still; the toppling houses join one another, so that only here and there

can one see a glimmer of pale light, as if one
were at the bottom of a well.

My door, which, in the darkness, I have not
yet learnt to enter without knocking my head,
gives access to something which is darker even
than the street : a staircase, there straight away
as soon as one enters ; a turret staircase, winding upwards on itself. It is so narrow that the
shoulders graze the walls on each side ; it is
steep as a ladder ; the steps are paved with
mosaics worn by the Arab slippers ; the walls
are blackened by the dirt of many human
generations, worn by the rubbing of hands,
and uneven as those of caverns. As we ascend,
we encounter at intervals bolted doors let into
disquieting recesses full of debris, of spiders'
webs and dust.

At last, at the height of what might be a
second storey, we reach a passage cut off by two
iron-mounted doors which seems, by its direction, to lead away from the street (but that,
indeed, is a matter of no importance, since there
are no windows and the street is black). It is
impossible to figure out the plan of a Fez house ;
they are generally intermixed one with another. Thus the ground floor, and perhaps
the first storey, of mine form part of a neighbouring house which I shall never enter.

At the end of this passage we reach the light

again, and the cold wind of out of doors; we enter a large room, with bare walls, cracked and dirty. The floor is tiled, and the high ceiling of cedarwood, carved with arabesques, has a large square opening, which discloses the grey sky; through this opening falls the cold rain, making a little trickling noise on the tiled floor; through this opening, during the day, descended a mournful light, and through it now descends the cold darkness of the night.

On to this interior court open two high folding doors of cedarwood, facing one another. They lead to symmetrical apartments, very high of ceiling, with cracked walls; one is mine and the other will be occupied to-morrow by Selem and Mohammed, my valets.

This same arrangement obtains in all Moroccan habitations: these same large folding doors, on each side of a court open to the sky, from which the house obtains all its light. The doors are not shut till after nightfall—for the simple reason that as soon as they are closed there is pitch darkness within; and, as they are massive, immense and hard to open, in each of the folds is provided a little ogival exit, which is like a kind of human cat's-hole, delicately framed with arabesques. It is the same everywhere, in the palace of the Sultan as well as in the dwelling of the humblest of his subjects.

. . . .

With a bar of iron a yard long, I bolted the great doors of my chamber, as is the custom at close of day. Then, through one of my little festooned cat's-holes, I issued forth, lantern in hand, to make a round of exploration in my house still little known to me. First, I descended by my spiral staircase to bar prudently the low entrance that communicates with the street; then, passing to the upper storeys, I was startled at my discoveries; other little passages, other dilapidated rooms, irregular in form and encumbered with debris, planks, old riding-saddles, pack-saddles for mules, dead fowls, and fowls that were alive.

It is a situation that very rarely falls to the lot of a European, to dwell thus in a house of his own in the holy city of Fez. In the first place, Europeans only come hither as part of an embassy, and, in such cases, are quartered in a palace set apart by the Sultan, which they are not allowed to leave without an armed escort. Even supposing that a " Nazarene " (as the Arabs call us) contrived to gain admittance alone, he would run grave risk of dying of hunger in the street; for at no price would a Mussulman consent to let him even the meanest lodging, or to prepare for him the simplest meal. But it happens that here at Fez there is a permanent French mission : three officers engaged in the instruction of the troops and an army doctor, Dr L*** (of whom, doubtless, I shall often have occasion to speak). With the English ex-colonel already mentioned, and an Italian officer in charge of an arms factory, they comprise the whole European colony of the town. Under the supreme protection of the Sultan, they are not in any way disturbed, and are able, in observing certain precautions, to go almost freely into the streets. By an imperial order, the chief kaids of the various wards have compelled the inhabitants, who submitted with an ill grace, to let to each of them a house ; and Dr L*** at this time, as a result of circumstances which I do not pretend to know, found himself in possession of two ; he offered one of them to me ; and it is thanks to him that I am going to live at Fez in circumstances of very exceptional liberty.

And now, barricaded finally for the night, my two cat's-holes closed, I am alone in my room, cold in spite of my burnous. I hear the rain falling, the gutters leaking, the wind blowing as in winter—and from time to time, from a distant mosque, comes the chanting of prayers. Very dilapidated and very dreary my large room seems, with its bare walls, cracked from ceiling to floor, whitewashed some centuries ago, and embellished now with the grey lace-work of spiders' webs.

In two of the corners, mysterious little doors lead to cavernous lofts. The floor, paved as everywhere with mosaic-work, will be a pretty thing to-morrow, when I have had it washed and freed from its thick layer of dust, but it will be the only one in my dwelling.

My furniture consists of a large Rabat carpet, faded in colour and ancient in design; a camp mattress placed on this carpet and covered with a Moroccan blanket; a little table and a tall brass candlestick. My clothes are already Arab from head to foot. And caftans and burnouses which a Jew came and sold me this evening are hung on nails, all ready for the interdicted promenades of to-morrow. There is nothing European about me except the pen with which, and the white paper on which, I write. The needy *tholbas*, who follow the courses of Karaouin, must, in their privacy, be equipped in some such way as I.

I review in my mind the swift succession of circumstances that has led me, as by some guiding thread stretched in advance, to this strange dwelling. First, my sudden and

unforeseen departure for Morocco.   Then those
twelve days on horseback, during which a
little of France followed me still: the gay
travelling companions with whom I was re-
united for the meals under the tent, talking
of things of the present century, forgetting
almost together the sombre country into which
we were penetrating.   Then our extravagant
entry of this morning into Fez, to the sound
of the tabours and bagpipes.   Then, suddenly,
my separation from the rest of the embassy;
my arrival in the rain at this ruinous shelter,
and my absolute solitude throughout the
afternoon.

These transformations, these translations
into the life of a foreign country, have always
been my chosen amusement, my chief resource
against the monotony of existence.   And to-
night I try to beguile myself with this Arab
costume, with the thought that I dwell in the
very heart of the holy city, in an inaccessible
little house.   But, somehow, it will not do;
over all, in spite of me, is a pervading sadness
that I had not looked for; a longing for the
firesides of France; an almost childish home-
sickness, which spoils for me the charm of this
novel strangeness.   I feel the shroud of Islam
falling upon me from all sides, enveloping me
in its heavy, ancient folds, with never a corner

raised to let in the air of other parts, and I find it much heavier to bear than I would have believed. Perhaps the fault lies a little in the deathlike aspect of this dwelling, in the little drops that fall from the ceiling with so desolate a little noise; in the voices chanting in minor, from the height of the minarets, at night. But truly one stifles, during the first few days, to feel around one the maze of these narrow little streets, and the presence of all these people, disdainful or hostile, who only tolerate you in their town under compulsion, and would willingly leave you to die like dogs by the wayside; and all these gates of the wards solidly shut; shut also the gates of the great ramparts imprisoning the whole; and beyond, the darkness of the wild campaign, more inhospitable even than the town, without roads by which one might flee and roamed by murderous tribes.

CHAPTER XXI

16th April.

THE first night passed in this house was as dismal as it well could be. Constantly those same sounds : the wind, the rain, the distant prayers.

About two o'clock in the morning the old doors of the staircases and passages were so shaken, with such a rattling of iron, that I thought I was invaded. And I made the round of my dwelling. But, no, nobody ; nothing but wind, and sudden squalls—and the bolts always in place.

When I awakened again it was to see the daylight filtering through the cracks of the great cedar doors. Barefooted, on the carpet that covers my tiled floor, I went first and opened one of the little ogival cat's-holes and looked up at the sky through the gaping opening in the roof ; still, obstinately, the same wintry sky, from which a fine, gentle rain continued to fall ; a cold wind, as in the countries of the north, blew upon my face. And in the light, at once wan and clear, that came with the rain from above, the antiquity, the desolation, the dilapidation of my house seemed even more extreme than before. The glazed mosaics of the floor, wet and cleansed, were alone in their fresh colours.

. . . .

The morning is passed in trying on robes of ceremony. One Edriss, an Algerian Mussulman domiciled in Morocco, whom Dr L*** has procured to act as my guide, brings for my selection cloth caftans of divers colours, rose, golden, nasturtium, dark blue; and sashes and turbans, and long silken cords to hold the poniard and the alms-bag in which every true believer carries, hung from the neck, a little manuscript commentary on the sacred books; and, finally, long veils of white transparent wool to be worn over all and subdue the colours.

He instructs me afterwards in the very difficult art of draping these veils in the proper manner. They are swathed two or three times about the body, taking in the arms, the head, the loins, and to their arrangement the whole toilet is subordinated.

Apart from any idea of disguise it is, of course, the case that the Arab costume is indispensable at Fez to anyone who wishes to go about at all freely and to see the life of the inhabitants at close quarters.

. . . .

Three o'clock in the afternoon.

There comes a knock at my door. I know who it is and descend to open, garbed now in a very simple Arab costume, in white wool a little soiled, such as one might see on passers-by in the streets. I find, below, three mules waiting, their heads set in the direction we are to follow, on account of the impossibility of turning between these high walls which almost touch each other. One of these mules is held by a groom, and, although it is a day of purification and retreat, I climb into the high-peaked, red-clothed saddle. The other two are mounted by personages in long burnouses, one of whom is Edriss, and the other, looking to-day like a real Bedouin, is Captain H. de V***, one of the members of the embassy, who is not " purifying " himself to-day any more than I. He is, for that matter, the constant companion of my excursions, and this country has the same kind of fascination for him as it has for me. We set out, the three of us, without exchanging a word, as for a prearranged goal. A fine rain is still falling from the lowering, misty sky.

For a long time we march in line, in the persistent rain which adds to the mournfulness of this labyrinth of dark little streets. More often than not we are in water, or liquid mud, up to the knees of our beasts, which trip over stones, sink into holes, and a score of times are on the point of falling.

Often we have to double in two, under arches so low that we are in danger of breaking our heads. Continually we have to stop, to take refuge in doorways, or to retire until we come to a turning, in order to allow other laden mules to pass, and horses and donkeys.

We go through covered bazaars, where reigns perpetually a kind of semi-twilight; there we are jostled by men and things of every sort; we crush passers-by against the houses, and, all the time, our stirrups grate against the old walls. At length we reach the goal of our journey: a large court of evil aspect, old, decrepit, like all else in Fez, and surrounded by massive porches which give it the appearance of a prison-yard: it is the slave-market—which Christians are not supposed to see.

It is empty to-day, this market; we have been ill informed; there have been no arrivals from the Soudan, apparently, for there will not be a soul to sell, they tell us, for another two or three days.

So, following Edriss, we continue on our way, still without speaking, in the maze of streets which seem to us to grow narrower and darker as we proceed.

And now a great murmur of voices reaches us, of voices praying and chanting together, in a rhythm that never changes, with an immense devotion. At the same time, in the dark labyrinth, appears a burst of luminous whiteness; it comes from a large ogival gateway, before which Edriss, our guide, who has greatly slackened speed, turns and looks at us. We interrogate him with an imperceptible sign : " That is it, isn't it ? " In the same manner, by a wink of his eye, he answers : " Yes ! " And we pass as slowly as may be, in order to see better.

For *that* is Karaouin, the holy mosque, the Mecca of all Moghreb, where, for the last ten years, a war has been preached against the infidels, and whence, every year, issue those fanatical doctors, who spread over Morocco, into Algeria, Tunis, Egypt, even into the heart of the Sahara and the black Soudan. Its vaults re-echo night and day, perpetually, with the same sound of chanting and prayer. It is capable of holding twenty thousand people; 'tis as extensive as a town. For centuries riches of every sort have been accumulated there, and within its confines happen things of uttermost mystery. Through the great ogival gateway we perceive indefinite distances of columns and arcades, all of exquisite form,

scooped out and carved and festooned with the
marvellous art of the Arabs. Thousands of
lanterns and girandoles hang from the vaults,
and all is of a snowy whiteness, which sheds a
kind of radiance into the gloom of the long
aisles. A multitude of faithful in burnouses
is prostrate on the ground, on the pavement
of bright coloured mosaics ; and the murmur
of religious chants uprises, continuous, monotonous, like the sound of the sea.

For fear of betraying ourselves, on a day
of obligatory quarantine, we dare not speak
to one another, nor stop, nor even gaze too
curiously.

But we are going to make the tour of the
immense mosque, which has full a score of
gates, and we shall see it again from other
aspects.

We go round it in semi-darkness, by a kind
of narrow roundway, sinking into mud, filth,
decaying refuse of every sort. Outside we see
nothing but the high, black walls, dilapidated,
toppling, against which lean the age-old houses
of the neighbourhood.

With a vague kind of awe, we slacken speed
every time we pass before one of the gates ;
the sanctuary then for a moment sends us its
white luminousness and its sound of pious
voices. It is so large that we cannot well

K

distinguish the plan of the whole. Its arcades are of an infinite variety, some tall and slender, carved with unimagined festoons, denticulated with clusters of stalactites; others in the form of multiple-leaved trefoils, of lofty arches, of ogives.

And always, on the ground, on the mosaics, the crowd of prostrate burnouses, murmuring the eternal prayers.

We shall often see Karaouin again, no doubt, during our stay in Fez, but I do not think it will ever make a more profound impression on us than at this first view furtively snatched on a day on which it was forbidden.

CHAPTER XXII

17th April.

WE are to be presented to the Sultan this morning, having been absolved from one of the days of quarantine.

At half-past eight we are all assembled, in gala dress, in the Moorish court of the house where dwell the Minister and his suite.

Arrives the " introducer of ambassadors," a colossal, bull-necked mulatto carrying a huge, battered cudgel. (To perform these functions one of the most giant-like men in the empire is always chosen.)

Four personages in long white robes enter in his train, and remain motionless behind him, armed each with a cudgel, similar to his own, which they hold, as a drum-major his baton, at arm's-length. These fellows are simply to clear a way for us through the crowd.

When it is time for us to mount, we cross the garden of orange-trees, on which the fine wintry rain inseparable from our journey continues to fall, and make our way to the low doorway that opens on to the street. One by one our horses are brought up ; they are unable either to turn or pass two abreast, so narrow is the street. And we mount the beasts at hazard as they come, hastily and in no sort of order.

We are some distance from the palace, and have to pass through those same quarters of the town by which we came the day before yesterday on our way hither. Ahead of us the cudgels descend, this way and that, on obstructive groups, and we are surrounded by a hedge of witless soldiers clothed all in red, who are constantly getting in the way of our horses, and whose bayonets, reaching just to the level of our eyes, are a permanent menace in the sudden turnings and congestions of the streets.

As on the day of our entry, we traverse the vacant ground which separates Fez-the-Old from Fez-the-New, the rocks, the aloes, the caves, the tombs, the ruins, and the heaps of putrefying beasts above which birds are wheeling.

And at last we arrive before the outer wall of the palace, and, through a large ogival gateway, enter into the Courtyard of Ambassadors.

This courtyard is so immense that I know no town in the world that possesses one of like dimensions. It is surrounded by high intimidating walls with pointed battlements, flanked by grim square bastions—as are the ramparts of Stamboul, of Damietta and Aigues Mortes—but here there is something even more dilapidated, more disquieting, more sinister. The rank grass grows everywhere about, and in the middle is a swamp in which frogs are croaking. The sky is wild and dark; clouds of birds escape from the embattled towers and whirl in the air.

The place seems empty, despite the thousands of men who are ranked here on the four sides, at the foot of the old walls. They are the same personages always, and the same colours. On one side, a white multitude in burnouses and hoods; on the other, a red multitude, the troops of the Sultan, having with them their musicians in long robes of orange and green and violet and nasturtium and golden-yellow. The central part of the immense courtyard into which we advance is completely deserted. All this crowd seems Lilliputian, at this so great distance, huddled at the foot of the crushing, embattled walls.

By one of its bastions the courtyard communicates with the precincts of the palace. This bastion, less dilapidated than the others, and dressed with whitewash, has two exquisite large ogival gateways framed with blue and rose arabesques; and it is through one of these arches that the sovereign will appear.

We are asked to dismount—for none is privileged to remain on horseback in the presence of the Chief of the Faithful—and our horses are led away. On foot now, all of us, on the wet grass, in the mud.

There is a movement amongst the troops; red soldiers and multi-coloured musicians advance in a double line, and form a wide avenue, from the centre of the courtyard where we stand to the bastion beyond, through which the Sultan is to come, and all eyes are now turned towards the arabesque-framed gateway awaiting the saintly apparition.

It is a full two hundred yards from us, this gateway, so immense is the courtyard, and through it, first of all, come viziers and other grand dignitaries; dark faces and long, grizzled beards; on foot, all of them, to-day, like us, and walking slowly in the whiteness of their veils and flowing burnouses. Almost all these personages are known to us already, for we saw them the day before yesterday, on our arrival; but they seemed more imposing then, mounted on their superb horses. Comes also the Kaid Belail, the black jester of the Court, his head still crowned with its fantastic, dome-shaped turban; he advances alone, swaying and swaggering, his gait strangely disquieting, leaning on an enormous loaded

bludgeon ; and there is something indescribably
sinister and mocking in his whole person ; he
seems to glory in the consciousness of the
extreme favour he enjoys.

The rain is still threatening ; storm-clouds,
driven by a high wind, scud across the sky,
which is flecked with clouds of birds and
shows, here and there, patches of that intense
blue which alone indicates the country of light
in which we are. All around, the walls, the
towers, bristle with their pointed battlements,
which have the appearance of rows of sharp-
toothed combs ; they seem gigantic, enclosing
us on all sides, as in a citadel of excessive,
fantastic dimensions ; time has endued them
with an extraordinary golden-grey colour ; they
are cracked, riven, tottering ; they produce
in the mind the impression of an antiquity
lost in deepest night. Two or three storks
perched on the points of battlements gaze down
upon the crowd ; and a mule, climbed, goodness
knows how, on to one of the towers, with its
high-peaked, red-clothed saddle, gazes down
too.

Through this door, framed in blue and pink
arabesques, upon which our attention is more
and more concentrated, issue now some fifty
little negro slaves, in red robes and muslin
surplices, for all the world like choir-boys.

They advance clumsily, huddled together like a flock of sheep.

Then six magnificent white horses, all saddled and harnessed in silk, are led out, rearing and prancing.

Then a gilt coach, in the style of Louis Quinze, unlooked for in such a setting, quaintly incongruous, ridiculous even amid all this rude grandeur (the solitary carriage, be it said, existing in Fez, a present to the Sultan from Queen Victoria).

Some minutes more of waiting and silence. Suddenly, a tremor of religious awe passes along the line of soldiers. The band, with its drums and huge brass instruments, strikes up a deafening, mournful air. The fifty little black slaves start running, running, seized by a sudden madness, spreading out fanwise like a flight of birds, like a swarm of bees. And beyond, in the half light of the ogive, upon which our eyes are fixed, mounted on a superb white horse led by four slaves, appears a tall, white, brown-faced mummy, veiled completely in muslin. Above his head is borne a red parasol of ancient shape, such as might have belonged to the Queen of Sheba, and two huge negroes, one in a pink robe, the other in a blue, wave fly-flaps before the august countenance.

And while this strange cavalier advances

towards us, almost shapeless, but imposing
nevertheless, in his cloud of snowy veils, the
band, as if in exasperation, breaks into ever
louder lamentations, on notes more strident still;
gives out a slow, disconsolate, religious hymn,
accompanied, out of time, by a terrific beating
of drums. The mummy's horse prances in
frenzy, and is with difficulty restrained by its
four black slaves. And from this music, so
mournful, so unimagined, the nerves receive
an indescribable impression of anguish.

And here now, come to a stop quite near us,
is the last authentic descendant of Mohammed,
bastardised with Nubian blood. His costume,
like a cloud of fine woollen muslin, is of
immaculate whiteness. His horse, too, is pure
white; his large stirrups are of gold; his
silken saddle and harness are of very pale water-
green, delicately broidered with golden-green
paler still. The slaves who lead his horse,
the one who bears the huge red parasol, and
the two—the pink and the blue—who wave the
white napkins to drive from about the sovereign
imaginary flies, are Herculean negroes, fiercely
smiling; all of them are old, and their white
and grey beards stand out sharply against the
black of their cheeks. And this ceremonial
of another age harmonises with this music of
lamentation, is framed with perfect fitness by

these immense surrounding walls, which up-
raise in the air their dilapidated battlements.

This man, who has been brought before us
with such pomp and circumstance, is the last
true representative of a religion, of a civilisation,
in way of dying. He is the very personification
of old Islam ; for, as is well known, pure Mussulmans consider the Sultan of Stamboul an almost
sacrilegious usurper and turn their eyes and
their prayers towards Al Moghreb, where
dwells, for them, the true successor of the
Prophet.

What good purpose can be served by a
mission to such a sovereign, immobilised, like
his people, in old human dreams that have
almost disappeared from the earth ? We are
absolutely incapable of understanding one
another ; the distance between us is almost
as great as that which would separate us from a
caliph of Cordova or Baghdad, come suddenly
to life again after a thousand years of sleep.
What do we want with him, and why have we
made him come out of his impenetrable palace ?

His brown, parchment face, framed by the
white muslins, has features regular and noble ;
and dead eyes that show the white below the
pupil half hidden by the eyelid ; his expression
is an excessive melancholy, a supreme lassitude,
an uttermost weariness. He seems gentle, and

is really so if we may believe those who live in contact with him—too much so, the people of Fez say : he does not lop off heads enough for the holy cause of Islam. But it is, no doubt, a relative gentleness, such as might have been understood amongst us in the Middle Ages, a gentleness that does not shrink unduly from the shedding of blood, when occasion requires, nor from a row of human heads stuck garland-wise above the beautiful ogives at the entrance to a palace. Assuredly he is not cruel ; with those kind, melancholy eyes of his he could not be so ; in the just exercise of his divine power he sometimes punishes severely, but, it is said, he likes much better to pardon. He is priest and warrior, and he is both to excess ; penetrated, as might be a prophet, with his celestial mission, chaste in the midst of his seraglio, faithful to the most rigorous religious observances and fanatical by heredity, he seeks to model himself as far as possible on Mohammed. One may read all this, indeed, in his eyes, in his handsome countenance, in his majestically upright carriage. Such as he is, we cannot hope, in our epoch, either to understand or judge him ; but, such as he is, he is beyond all question grand and imposing.

And there, before us, people of another world brought near him for a few minutes, he betrays

an indefinable shyness, almost timidity, which
gives his personality a singular and altogether
unexpected charm.

.   .   .   .

The Minister presents his credentials to the
Sultan, in a velvet pouch embroidered with gold,
which is taken by one of the fly-flickers. Then
the brief customary speeches are exchanged :
first that of the Minister ; afterwards the reply
of the Sultan, affirming his friendship for
France, in a low, weary, condescending, very
distinguished voice. Then our individual pre-
sentations, our salutes, to which the sovereign
replies by a courtly inclination of the head—
and it is over. The Chief of the Faithful has
shown himself enough for Nazarenes such as we.
The black slaves turn about the beautiful silk-
harnessed horse ; the Sherifian mummy shows
his back to us, looking like a great phantom in
vaporous shrouds. The band which, during
the speeches, had dropped to an undertone,
breaks again into a mournful crescendo ; another orchestra, of bagpipes and tabours, yelps
at the same time on notes of even greater
stridency ; quite near us, the gun recom-
mences to boom, frightening the horses : the
Sultan's rears and kicks, endeavouring to dislodge its snowy mummy, who remains impassible ; and all the others, the six superb led

beasts, break away in furious bounds; the one
in the gilt coach stands fully upright on its
hind legs; the fifty little black slaves renew
their mad, streaming flight—which is a thing
of etiquette every time the master rides abroad.

In the frenzied crescendo of the musicians,
to the heavy booming of the gun, the cortège of
the Caliph draws rapidly away from us, like an
apparition put to flight by an excess of movement and noise; it is swallowed up in the
darkness of the ogive bordered with blue and
rose arabesques. We see a last effort by the
beautiful horse to dislodge its impassible white
cavalier; then all disappears, including the
red parasol and the fifty choir-boys, who surge
through the gateway like a wave. A shower
begins to fall and we run now through the tall,
wet grass to find our horses, in the midst of a
sudden disbanding of negro soldiers clothed
in red, of all the pitiful army of monkeys. A
strange disorder and tumult succeeds the calm
of a few moments ago in the gigantic square of
walls and ruined towers.

. . . .

At length we are mounted on horseback
again, to go, according to custom after the
reception of an embassy by the Sultan, to
visit the gardens of the palace with the viziers.

We pass through other crenellated ramparts

tremendously high, through other ogival gateways with folding, iron-mounted gates, through
other walled courtyards, the ground of which
is broken by sinks and quagmires. All this is
extraordinarily old, all this is in ruins, imposing
always and sinister. The most impressive of
these courtyards is a rectangle some two or
three hundred yards in length, bounded by
embattled walls that are at least fifty feet high.
At the two ends of this courtyard open, sym-
metrically, large gateways, coated with whitewash like all the entrances to the palace, and
framed, as always, with blue and pink arabesques.
And each of these gateways is flanked by four
enormous embattled towers, which, like the
ramparts, have been left with the sombre
colour given them by the centuries. They
mount in steps, the end towers rising much
higher than those of the centre. Words cannot
tell the savage aspect of the place, nor the
grimness, nor the mournful monotony of these
high walls, of all these battlements outlined
on the sky.

Afterwards we pass between two rows of
high grey walls, still unfinished, along a kind
of lofty corridor, which the Sultan is having
made, in order that his women may be able to
pass into the gardens without being seen from
any point, whether from the terraces or the

surrounding mountains. We hear there a kind of religious choir, accompanied from time to time by a sound that resembles a muffled blow struck on many drums at once. One might think it was a funeral service in a mosque— but, in simple fact, it is the workmen busy in a row on the summit of a wall of beaten earth.

They sing, in adagio minor, a woeful lamentation, and, at the end of each strain, which lasts for a full fifteen seconds, strike a blow on their building, to harden the clay, with one of those heavy wooden pestles known as " demoiselles "; that is the whole of their work, which will continue in this manner until nightfall.

They watch us coming, and we, on our part, also watch them, amused and wondering. The whole performance seems a mockery, a thing done for a wager. But in no wise: these fellows here are serious. It appears indeed that whenever men work by the day for the Sultan, they adopt this slow solemnity.

Having passed through the enclosure they are building, we turn back, pursued by their trailing canticle, to look at them again, and we expected this time to see them from the back. But, by a comical general movement, they, too, have turned round, in order to follow us with their eyes; and they continue to work to the same cadence, with the same unbelievable slowness.

One last gateway, and we enter the gardens of the Sultan—orchards rather; large, neglected orchards, enclosed within ruinous walls; but orchards of orange-trees, which are exquisite in their forlornness and perfumed with a most suave fragrance. The avenues are sheltered by bowers of vine branches, and paved with white marble, with venerable flags, worn and green with age. The trees, very old, bear at one and the same time their golden fruit and their white blossom. Below grow the rank weeds. In places, swamps, savannahs.

Here and there are old, melancholy kiosks, where, it appears, the Sultan comes to rest with his women. Their arabesques are effaced by whitewash.

There emerges from the whole a melancholy as of a graveyard. How many beautiful cloistered creatures, chosen, in the bloom of youth, from amongst the fairest of all Moghreb, must this grove of orange-trees have seen pass, grow weary, fade and die !

CHAPTER XXIII

18th April.

IT is one of the complications of existence in this city that you are never able to go out alone, even in Arab costume ; in the first place, you would risk an unpleasant adventure, and in the second, and this more especially, it would not be seemly, for decorum requires that you should always be preceded by one or two domestics, stick in hand, to make a way for you. Nor can you venture forth on foot, again out of respect for convention, and also because you would sink to the knees in mud, and be crushed against the close-set walls by the laden mules and handsome, haughty cavaliers. And then, such is the indolence of the servants, that you are a prisoner for three parts of the time in your own house, for want of a mount of any sort saddled at the stated hour.

Every morning I have luncheon in the Minister's house with the other officers of the embassy. But it would be impossible for me to dine there of evenings, on account of the return after nightfall, when the gates of the wards are shut, cutting off communication between us.

But I have for neighbour, almost next door to me, Dr L***—him to whom I am indebted for the loan of the house in which I live—and we dine together every evening. I go to his house on foot, walking with legs wide apart, my slippers touching the walls on the two sides of the street, in order to avoid the black stream in the middle. At his door, which is as low and dark as my own, I generally bump my forehead as I enter. And, later on, I return by lantern-light, preceded by my two domestics, Mohammed and Selem, and at eight o'clock barricade myself in my venerable house. Mohammed and Selem occupy the rooms symmetrical with mine on the opposite side of my interior court. Behind their cedar doors, which are absolutely identical with mine, they make tea throughout the night and sing songs with guitar accompaniment. In the morning when I open my door, opposite to me they open theirs, wish me good-morning, put on their burnouses and go out for a walk. Neither by bribes nor threats shall I ever succeed in making them serve me the least bit better. Generally, they leave me alone in my dwelling, obliged, when, in the distance, I hear the sound of the heavy knocker of my door, obliged myself to descend my turret staircase in order to open to the visitor.

If I relate these trifling things, it is because they give some idea of the difficulties that beset a European stranded in Fez, even when, like me, he finds himself there in circumstances of exceptional comfort.

.   .   .   .

This morning, as yesterday afternoon, there are official visits to be paid to various great personages. Still the same fine cold rain, which has accompanied us since the setting out and, yesterday, made the gardens of the Sultan seem so melancholy.

At the houses of the viziers and ministers, whither we repair on horseback through the dark and tortuous little streets, we are received in those courts open to the sky which constitute the greatest luxury of the houses of Fez : courts all paved with mosaics, all ornamented with arabesques, and surrounded by elaborately festooned arcades. At other times, it is at the bottom of those exquisitely mournful gardens, which are rather groves of orange-trees invaded by weeds, with avenues paved with white flagstones and shaded by bowers of vine branches ; the whole surrounded, needless to say, by those high prison walls which serve to render invisible the fair denizens of the harems.

The state dinners will not commence till next week; so far there are only luncheons, but luncheons worthy of Pantagruel, such as were those of our ancestors in the Middle Ages. On tables, or on the ground, are set large tubs of European or Japanese porcelain, heaped with fruits, shelled nuts, almonds, " gazelles' hoofs," preserves, dates, saffroned sweetmeats. Gauze veils, highly coloured and sequined with gold, cover these mountains of things, which would suffice for a couple of hundred people. Blue and rose-coloured decanters, richly painted and overlaid with gildings, contain a detestable water, earthy and fetid, which it behoves one not to drink. We sit down on carpets, on broidered cushions, or on European chairs of a past style, Empire or Louis Seize, and are waited upon by black slaves, or by kinds of janissaries armed with long, curved sabres, and coiffed in pointed tarbushes.

Never any coffee or cigarettes, for the Sultan has forbidden their use. In his edict against tobacco, he has even gone so far as to compare the depravity of the smoker's taste with that of a man who should partake of the flesh of a dead horse.

Nothing but tea, and the odorous, and a little intoxicating, smoke of that precious Indian wood, which is burnt before us in silver brasiers. Everywhere, the tall Russian samovars, and the same tea, flavoured with mint, with citron, and sweetened to excess.

Good form requires that one should partake of it three times, and the custom is a grievous one; for at each turn of the tray the cups used by the different guests become hopelessly mixed, and the dregs remaining in each are poured ruthlessly back into the tea-urn.

During these visits, needless to say, we never see the women; but we are constantly watched by them. Every time we turn we are sure to see, through some trefoil concealed in the arabesques of the wall, through some narrow loophole, or above the parapet of a terrace, pairs of long, painted eyes examining us curiously; they vanish, disappear into the shadow, as soon as our gaze meets theirs.

These Moroccan personages by whom we are received have all a distinguished air; in the folds of their soft, white veils they walk and move with nobility, with an indescribable aristocratic indolence and unconcerned tranquillity. For all that, one feels that they are of less worth than the common people, the bronzed, fearless folk of the open air. Riches, and the greed to acquire ever greater riches, and the subterfuges of politics, have spoilt them. At these first preliminary visits, the

Minister makes no mention of the business of
his mission; but one divines that it will be
long in the settling, at mere sight of these airs
of cunning and mistrust, of the feline half-
smiles of these white-robed men who never
answer but in gracious circumlocutions—who
seem never spontaneous, never sincere.

.   .   .   .

The son of the Grand Vizier is about to be
married, and since yesterday the whole of Fez
has resounded with the revelry of his nuptials.
In the dark little streets, interminable cortèges
come and go, preceded by tom-toms, wailing
bagpipes and musket shots. We met one, this
morning, of at least three hundred persons,
who fired their guns in the gloom of the little
vaulted passages, shaking all the old walls;
those marching at the head carried presents
on their heads: very voluminous things enveloped in silken fabric figured with gold.

The house of this vizier, when we visited him
in the afternoon, was decorated magnificently
for the great festival. In the court, all in
mosaics and filigree arabesques, were hung
innumerable girandoles almost touching one
another and masking absolutely the cloudy
vault of the sky; all the delicate carvings of the
walls were bedizened with fresh gold, fresh blue
and pink and green; and all around, up to the

height of the first storey, were placed magnificent hangings of red velvet, broidered, in relief, with gold ; those Arab hangings, the designs on which represent rows of arches, of festoons, like the doors of mosques.

In the apartments opening on to this court of honour was a display, in astonishing profusion, of hangings and cushions of brilliant and rare colours, interwoven with golden-yellows and golden-greens in a diversity of strange, almost religious, designs. Against this richness, the person of the Grand Vizier stood out all white, enveloped in simple muslins; his handsome feline countenance, changing, unreadable, framed in its grey beard.

The Minister asked to be allowed to see, not, to be sure, the bride, since she is still invisible even to her spouse, but the bridegroom and the young men of his suite.

The vizier smilingly consented, and led us through a garden to the house prepared for the new *ménage*; a house quite new, and still unfinished, but constructed in the immutable style of Granada and Cordova; an army of workmen was busy there, patiently carving the arabesques.

There, on divans, arranged around a large bare hall, a number of young men were seated, holding festival, with tea and sweetmeats and perfumed smoke: the gilded youth of Fez, the new generation, the future kaids and the future viziers, who will perhaps be called upon to see the overthrow of old Moghreb. Quite young, all of them, but etiolated, pale, gloomy and limp on their cushions. The son of the Grand Vizier, clothed in green (the bridegroom's colour), was seated apart from the rest in a corner, the gloomiest and limpest of all, wearing an air of absolute dejection, as if worn out with weariness and lassitude. At half the height of the large hall in which these young men were entertaining themselves, the smoke of the odorous Indian wood made, as it were, a pall of grey clouds.

CHAPTER XXIV

19th April.

IN a few hours, as commonly happens in this country, the sky has become clear, and there is now nothing in the air. In place of the grey clouds, which passed and passed again, darkening thoughts and things alike, is an immense void, profound and clear, which this evening is of an irisate blue, of a blue turning, on the horizon, to the green of aqua-marina. All around is a great splendour, a great festival, and a great magic of light.

In the wonderful hours of this close of the day, I climb to my terrace and sit there. The old fanatical and sombre town is bathed in the gold of all this sunlight; spread out at my feet, on a succession of hills and dales, it has taken on an aspect of unalterable and radiant peace; it looks almost smiling, almost pretty; I scarcely recognise it, so much has it changed; a kind of ruddy radiance sleeps on the immobility of its ruins. And the air has suddenly become warm and tranquil, giving an illusion of eternal summer.

Around me, in the foreground, are grouped

the flat roofs of the highest of the neighbouring houses : tops of cubes of stone, irregularly
placed, as if thrown at hazard. Between these
roofs and mine is emptiness ; although I can
distinguish with perfect clearness the smallest
details of their objects, the least cracks in the
walls, they are separated from me by a kind of
mist of light, which gives something of vague-
ness to their bases, rendering them almost
vaporous ; so that it seems as if they were
suspended in the air. And all these high
promenades become gradually thronged with
women, who appear one after another, rising
up, clothed in the costumes of idols, and coiffed
in the *hantouze* (a gilt mitre resembling the
hennin of the last days of our Middle Ages).

Beyond these neighbouring terraces, which
are those of houses built, like mine, on the
highest part of Old Fez—after another emptiness, another luminous mist, appears an infinite succession of more distant things, seen
through a kind of transparent gauze. First,
all the rest of Old Fez : a thousand terraces,
of a violet-grey, on which the fair aerial pro-
menaders seem no more than so many spots of
brilliant colour sprinkled over a monotonous
scattering of ruins. Above this uniformity of
cubes of stone rise a few slender palm-trees,
and, in addition, all the old square towers of

the mosques, with their coatings of yellow and green tiles, burnt by long centuries of sunshine, with their little cupolas, surmounted each with a golden sconce.

Of New Fez, which is farther away, I can see no more than the high, grim walls, enclosing the seraglios, the palaces, the courtyards of the Sultan. And a girdle of green gardens, of the most beautiful green of springtime, surrounds the great town; its old ramparts, its old bastions, its old formidable towers, are, as it were, drowned in fresh verdure.

It is clear, astonishingly clear. Despite this intangible vapour, which is rainbow-tinted in the depths and of a golden rose on the summits, I can see distant things as if they were quite near me, or as if my eyes, this evening, had acquired an unaccustomed penetration.

Beyond are Karaouin and Mulai-Edriss, the two great sacred mosques, the mere names of which, before my arrival, struck me with the awe of things of utmost mystery! I see, from above, their minarets, their roofs covered like those of the Alhambra with green tiles: seen thus, bathed in light, in the tranquillity of this brilliant sunshine, they seem to have lost their power to awe, they seem no longer to be formidable sanctuaries; and in the same way the great town itself, in the midst of its girdle of green gardens, so calm in the softness of this light of ruddy gold, has lost its gloomy, forbidding air, its air of mysterious immutability. It is difficult to imagine that this is indeed the walled heart of Islam, the lonely Mecca of Al Moghreb, without roads communicating with the rest of the world.

Farther on still, beyond the gardens and the ramparts, the gigantic circle of the mountains is bathed also in light. I can distinguish this evening the least of the valleys, the least of the recesses; as through a field-glass I can discern all that passes there. Here and there, caravans, infinitely little in the distance, are journeying towards the Soudan, or towards Europe. In the east, where the last rays of the sun fall full, is a region of cemeteries and ruins; the nearest slopes, in the neighbourhood of the town, are covered with the debris of walls, of *koubas* of saints, of little funerary domes, of innumerable tombs; and, as it is Friday (the Mussulman Sabbath), a day of pious visits to the dead, these cemeteries are thronged with people. Amongst the stones we can see the visitors moving about, in their greyish burnouses, looking, from afar off, like stones themselves, like moving stones. Above, the mountain tops are of an ardent rose-colour, with dark shadows absolutely blue. And higher still, and farther away, the great Atlas, capped in glistening snow, of a different kind of rose-colour, paler and more transparent, is outlined, like a clear-cut crystal, against the bright yellow which begins to encroach upon and to replace the disappearing blue of the sky.

In the west, a high, adjacent mountain rises like a jagged screen before the sun, casting its shadow over a part of the town. It is striated obliquely from summit to base, and, with its pointed crest, resembles a wave that might have risen there and become fixed for ever. One feels that behind it, on its farther slopes, one would still be in the full splendour of the sun; it is all edged and fringed with light.

Clouds of black birds wheel above the roofs, and large storks, also, pass in tranquil flight across the golden-green of the sky.

.   .   .   .

It is Good Friday, a day on which in our countries the still diffident spring is veiled usually in grey clouds; so much so, that the expression " Good Friday weather " has come to indicate an overcast, wind-tossed sky. But the town in which I am does not wear, does not recognise even, this mourning of the Christians, and basks voluptuously this evening in the calm, warm air under a sky in gala dress.

In the countries of Islam, the Friday, as

with us the Sunday, is for the people a day
of rest and toilet. And thus, this evening,
the women, more numerous than usual, and
more gaily attired, issue from the little doors
of the kinds of sentry-boxes which are the heads
of the staircases of the houses; emerge one after
another on to the roofs, shaking themselves like
birds, enamelling with their brilliant colours all
these grey terraces.

Grey, all these terraces, colourless rather, of a
dead, neutral, indifferent shade, which changes
with the weather and the light. Whitewashed
once upon a time, and rewhitened again and
again until they lost shape and sharpness under
the superimposed layers; then baked by the
sun, calcined by the burning heat, guttered
by the rains, until they have become almost
blackish. A little mournful, indeed, the high
promenades of these women. And everywhere,
on my own terrace as well as on those of my
fair neighbours, the old walls on which we lean,
and which serve as a parapet to prevent us
from falling into the void, are crowned with
lichen, with saxifrage and tiny yellow flowers.

They walk about in groups, these women,
or sit down to talk on the ledges of the walls,
their legs hanging over the courtyards and
streets, or lie down, nonchalantly reclining,
their upraised arms under their heads. They

climb from one house to another, with the help
sometimes of a ladder, or of planks forming an
improvised bridge. The negresses, sculpturesque
creatures, wear in their ears large silver rings;
their robes are white or pink; scarves frame the
blackness of their faces; their laughing voices
sound like rattles, in droll, monkey-like merriment. The Arab women, their mistresses, wear
tunics figured with gold and veiled by embroidered net: the long, wide sleeves disclose
their shapely bare arms encircled with bracelets;
high waistbands of silk laminated with gold, as
stiff as cardboard bands, support their breasts;
on all the foreheads there are headbands, formed
of a double row of gold sequins, or of pearls
or precious stones, and above is placed the
hantouze, the tall mitre, swathed always in
scarves of golden gauze, the ends of which hang
loose and float behind, mingling with the mass
of unbound hair; they walk with the head
thrown back, the lips open, showing the white
teeth; they sway their hips with a little
exaggeration and with a voluptuous slowness;
their eyes, naturally very large and very dark,
are joined together and extended as far as the
temples with antimony; many are painted,
not with carmine, but with pure vermilion, as
if in some barbarous attempt to outdo nature;
their cheeks seem thickly coated with minium,

and on their arms, on their foreheads, appear blue tattooings.

All this splendour, which is completely veiled in greyish-white whenever it is a matter of walking, like mysterious phantoms, in the labyrinth of muddy little streets below, is here displayed complacently in broad daylight. This town, which seems so dull and dark to one who passes through it without raising his head, unfolds all its fashionable feminine life of an evening on its roofs, in the golden hours of the close of the day. Mistresses and slaves, without distinction of caste, walk about pell-mell, laughing together, and often arm-in-arm, with an appearance of complete equality.

And there are no veils on these faces, which in the street are so carefully hidden, for men are not supposed ever to mount to the terraces of Fez.

I indeed am doing a very improper thing in remaining seated on mine. But I am a foreigner; and I am able to pretend that I do not know.

Meanwhile the gold is darkening, fading on all sides; the kind of roseate radiance which shone on the old religious town gradually ascends again towards the upper strata of the air; the summits of the towers and the highest of the terraces alone continue to shine; a violet shadow begins to spread in the distances, in the low-lying places, in the valleys. Soon will sound the hour of the fifth and last prayer of the day, the sacred hour, the hour of Moghreb. And all the heads of the women are turned towards the venerable mosque of Mulai-Edriss, as if waiting for some religious signal.

There is for me a magic and an indescribable charm in the mere sound of this word: Moghreb. Moghreb; it signifies, at one and the same time, the west, the setting sun, and the hour of sunset. It designates, too, the empire of Morocco, which is the most westerly of all the countries of Islam, and the part of the earth where has come to die, in slowly gathering gloom, the great religious impulse given to the Arabs by Mohammed. Above all, it is the name of that last prayer which, from one end of the Mussulman world to the other, is said at this hour of the evening—a prayer which starts from Mecca, and, in a general prostration, is propagated in a slow trail across the whole of Africa, in measure as the sun declines—to cease only in the presence of the ocean, in those last Saharan dunes where Africa itself ends.

. . . .

The gold continues to fade. Fez is already plunged in the shadow of its great mountains; the part of it that is near us is drowned in the

M

violet vapour which has risen, little by little, like an incoming tide; and the distant parts can scarcely be discerned at all. Alone, the snows on the summit of the Atlas preserve for a last dying minute their ruddy glitter.

Then a white flag is run up on the minaret of Mulai-Edriss.

As if in sudden answer, on all the other minarets of the other mosques other similar white flags appear.

" Allah Akbar ! "

An immense cry of blind faith resounds through the entire town.

" Allah Akbar ! "

On your knees, all ye faithful ! On your knees in the mosques, on your knees in the streets, on your knees at the threshold of your doors, on your knees in the fields : it is the holy hour of Moghreb !

" Allah Akbar ! "

From the height of all the mosques the muezzins, putting their hands to their mouths, repeat the long religious lamentation to the four cardinal points, trailing mournfully their shrill voices, in the manner of wolves a-howling.

.   .   .   .

All is quiet—the sun has set—a vapour of a deeper violet accentuates still more the emptiness between the terraces; they seem to separate

themselves one from another, to recede from
me with their groups of women who now are
motionless. A silence falls upon the town,
after the immense prayer.

.   .   .   .

The night has fallen, the stars come out.
I can now distinguish nothing—nothing, save
that above, on a terrace overlooking mine, a
woman is standing, outlined in shadow at the
angle of the roof ; alone, superbly posed, her
hands behind her back, contemplating I know
not what, below, in the void.

CHAPTER XXV

20*th* *April*.

THERE was fighting, during the night, in the Sultan's camp (which is in course of formation under the walls of the town for the next expedition). It was about a mule that was claimed by two detachments. From midnight till one o'clock there was a continuous rattle of musket-shots. Some twenty men were wounded and four were slain. We saw the dead being carried away, grey heaps on a litter.

The glorious weather and the festival of light continue. The sky is of pure indigo blue and the heat increases. With the evil odours of the town are mingled puffs of suave perfume, which come from the orange blossom of the gardens. I have grown used to my little house, which no longer seems to me in any way sinister. In the part that I inhabit I have had the tiles cleaned and the walls refaced with whitewash. (In odd corners I discovered fresh little doors, leading to passages, niches, *oubliettes* ; excellent things if you wanted to make anyone disappear.) I find quite natural my little low door with its ironwork of the year 1000, and my narrow, dark street has ceased to frighten me. I have grown used to my neighbourhood, and my neighbours have grown used to me, and cease to stare at me. Irregular though it be and embarrassing to the fair ladies of the neighbourhood I begin to spend much of my time on my terrace, especially at the sacred hour of Moghreb, when the white flags are hoisted on the mosques, when the muezzins appear high up on the minarets to chant the prayer, and the great mountains grow sombre in their evening tints of violet and rose.

I have found out who occupies the house that is so interlaced with mine. He is a person of substance, an Amin, something like a pay-master-general of the Sultan's army. The noise I hear so regularly every morning and every evening—it aroused my curiosity not a little— I find is the pounding of sugar and cinnamon bark to make sweets for his children, who are very numerous. The life of this land, so immured as it is, has undercurrents of perfect good nature when one comes to see it closely. In the evening, through the walls, I hear the voices of the children and wives of this Amin. They keep me company.

I have grown used to my long Arab robes, to the fashionable manner of holding my hands in my veils and of draping my burnous. And, very often, I return to trail my slippers in the purlieus of the mosque of Karaouin, in the labyrinth of the bazaar, which, in the bright sunshine, has taken on an aspect very different from that of the first days.

.   .   .   .

This evening, Captain H. de V***, my habitual companion, and I, garbed both as Arabs, came upon the slave-market. The mournful courtyard held not a soul. And when we asked if there was likely to be business doing soon—it is generally at nightfall, after the hour of the prayer of the Moghreb, that the slaves and buyers and sellers come—we were answered : " We know not, but that negress, in the corner there, is still for sale."

She was sitting, this negress, on the edge of one of those niches that have been hollowed out like dens in the thickness of the old walls; her head bowed down and enveloped in a grey veil, her face covered, she had an air of utter consternation. And when she saw us approaching, fearing no doubt lest she should be bought, she seemed to shrink still more. We made her get up, in order that we might see her, as is the custom with all merchandise : she was a girl of sixteen or eighteen years, half child, half woman, and her tearful eyes expressed a resigned but boundless despair. She wrung her veil with her two hands and kept her head bowed upon the ground. Oh ! how our hearts smote us at the sight of this poor little creature, who rose docilely to let herself be examined, and stood there, awaiting her lot. By her side, in the same niche, was an elderly woman, her veil carefully drawn across her face, who seemed by her appearance to belong to a superior class, despite her simple costume. It was her mistress, who had brought her hither to the market to sell her. We asked the price : five hundred francs. The woman tearfully, and with eyes as sad as those of her slave, explained to us that she had bought this child when she was quite little and had brought her up, but that now, having become a widow and poor, she was no longer able to support her and found herself obliged to part with her. And these two women awaited a purchaser, timidly, humbly, the one as hopeless as the other. It might have been a mother come to sell her child.

.   .   .   .

At Fez, needless to say, one goes not out at night unless one is forced to it. In the narrow, vaulted little streets, the darkness, after eight o'clock, is profound. One risks falling into sewers, into wells, into *oubliettes*, which stretch here and there their gaping mouths.

This evening, however, we have all to go to

the palace, and the order has been given to leave open the gates of the wards on the way.

.   .   .   .

We set out at half-past eight, from the Minister's house, on restive mules. The inevitable red soldiers, their bayonets fixed, escort us with large lanterns, the panels of which are shaped in the form of ogives like the doors of the mosques.

First we pass in a line through a neighbourhood of gardens, zigzagging in the darkness between low walls above which stretch the sweetly scented branches of orange-trees. Then through a corner of a covered bazaar; through winding streets, paved in breakneck fashion, where a few lights are still glimmering in the little, sleeping shops. Then a wide, black-dark street, between long ruinous walls. Some Arabs rolled for the night in their burnouses lie sleeping there on the ground, in company with dogs, and we all but trample them underfoot. Then at length the gates of the first enclosures of the palace, guarded by soldiers with naked sabres; the massive folds, strengthened by enormous bands of iron, have been left ajar against our coming. And we cross, by lantern-light, the immense courtyards already known to us; the deserted spaces with their sinks and quagmires, bounded by the gigantic walls which outline, against the starry sky, all their pointed battlements, like rows of black combs. And along our route guards are marshalled, sabre in hand. One feels that it is not a hospitable place that we are penetrating.

At length we reach the Courtyard of Ambassadors, the largest of all. The darkness here is more transparent, because there is more space, more distance. The frogs croak in noisy concert, assisted after their kind by a few nocturnal grasshoppers. Beyond, in the far background, are other lanterns perforated like our own, and towards these we direct our steps. They illuminate grave, white-robed personages who are awaiting us: the viziers and kaids of the palace.

We are going to display before them the presents we have brought for the ladies of the seraglio: clusters of electric flowers, electric jewels, stars and crescents, to be worn in the hair of the invisible fair ones. We are warned that the Sultan himself is roaming around us, in the great darkness that envelops us, in order to see without being seen; that perhaps, if he be interested, he may go so far as to show himself. We watch, therefore, the few rare torches that move about in the distances of the courtyard, expecting every minute his saintly apparition. But it is not to be; the Caliph,

insufficiently interested no doubt, shows himself
not.

The batteries take a long time to get ready ;
they seem to be actuated by a spirit of perverse-
ness. And all these little playthings of the nine-
teenth century which we have brought hither
light up with difficulty, shine no more brightly
than so many glow-worms, in the immense,
age-old darkness that surrounds us.

21st April.

Easter Sunday.—The weather is luminous and
splendid, increasingly warm ; the suave perfume
of the orange-trees and the odours of the dead
beasts hang heavily in the air.

It is delightful in the garden of the Minister's
house. We stay sitting there for a long time every
day after luncheon, in front of the old pavilion,
with its arabesques half effaced by whitewash ;
the large orange-trees, laden with white blossom
and golden fruit, stand out, above our heads,
against the crude blue of the sky ; and we hear,
with a kind of cool voluptuousness, the water
spurting from the marble basin and streaming
on to the mosaic pavement.

. . . .

All day long H. de V*** and I, clothed both
of us in Arab fashion, have haunted the bazaar ;
we mingle more and more freely in the crowds,

where no one any longer heeds us, so correct and natural have we become.

We are beginning to find our way without difficulty in this bazaar, in the labyrinth of these little streets roofed with vine branches or reed screens, where, between dark little shops glinting with arms and silks and gold, throng the white-hooded buyers.

.   .   .   .

This evening, to the slave-market, at the sacred and already twilight hour of Moghreb, is brought quite a band of little negresses, freshly captured in the Soudan and wearing still the gummed coiffures, the amulets and the necklaces of their native land. Some greybeards, richly garbed in robes of snowy whiteness, examine them, feel them, stretch their arms, open their mouths to look at their teeth. In the upshot they fail to find a buyer and the trader leads them away, a melancholy troop, with heads bowed down. They pass quite close to me, and, merely by their aspect, and their savour, they remind me of Senegal, bring back a whole world of dead memories.

.   .   .   .

On the roof of my house, in the last light of day, I watch the great storm-clouds slowly invade the sky, presaging the end of the fine weather. They are of the colour of tarnished copper, and below them, the thousands of terraces become grey, a cold grey almost blue.

How soon it has become familiar to me, this view of the town from above! No sound reaches me of rolling wheels, no din of machinery, nothing but a confused murmur of human voices, of neighings of horses, of the sounds of old-world crafts : the weaving of fabrics, or the hammering of metal.

Truly, I have come to know by heart all the little routine of the life of the evening on the summits of the houses. I know all my neighbours who, one after another, emerge from the little doors, and, sitting down, remain, spots of fantastic colour on the greyish uniformity, until that twilight hour when the green-clad towers of the mosques become grey themselves, and all is confused and blotted out. That fair lady yonder, generally in a blue robe with a yellow hennin, comes always followed by an orange-robed negress, who carries a little ladder to enable her mistress to mount to the neighbouring roof, behind which she disappears (? ? . . .). That other, in the direction of Karaouin, climbs without assistance, with much raising of her knees, and over-steps a street to reach a higher roof and join her friends, who number a full half-score, as many black as white. I know where the

storks—which snap their beaks, motionless on
their long stilts—I know where they have built
their nests. I even know the different cats
of the neighbourhood, which pay visits like
the women, climbing over terraces and leaping
over streets. And I know, too, these clouds
of black, yellow-billed birds, resembling our
blackbirds, which, while a glimmer of daylight
remains, chase one another, as martins do
with us, in wide, whirling circles.

 .   .   .   .

A *tholba* of the mosque of Karouin, a very
civil *tholba*, who evinces a condescending curiosity in things European, is sometimes the
companion of my idleness on the terraces ; but,
being a Mussulman and a citizen of Fez, he
hides himself in the shelter of the walls, so
that he may not be seen by the promenading
ladies. This evening he took me on to another
roof in order to show me my street, which I
had never seen from so great a height. At
the point to which we climbed, it was scarcely
more than six inches wide, so close together
were the houses at the top. Very easily could
we have overstepped it and gone to visit the
fair ladies of the neighbourhood : it seemed no
more than a crevice, a black fissure, deep at the
bottom of which, as in a well, passers-by, who
had the air of phantoms, trailed their slippers

through the dirt. And, in contrast, above on the roofs, all was light, glitter of gay costumes, merry chattering of women, careless ease, free air and space.

. . . .

He is really very modern, this *tholba*, very *studious* even, in his way of understanding youth, in his constant preoccupation with women and pleasure. Evidently he is an exceptional kind of *tholba*; and, through him, I shall soon be well versed in the gay life of this country.

I should never have imagined that Fez was the town in Africa where life in this kind may be most easily led. It is the case, however, that over and above the many holy persons, there is here a large number of merchants of every sort; a certain fever of gold, quite different, it is true, from ours, rages within its walls. Men, grown rich too quickly—on the return, for example, of a fortunate caravan from the Soudan—hasten to " enjoy life," and espouse a number of young women; ruined the following year, they divorce them and depart, abandoning the women to their own personal resources. And thus Fez is full of divorced wives who support themselves as best they can. Some live alone, with the toleration of the kaid of the district, and become fashionable ladies of equivocal sort in tall gilt tiaras. Others, fallen lower, group themselves under the patronage of some old matron. But the houses of these latter are dens of a dangerous kind, situated always above the Oued Fez (the river, running almost entirely underground, that feeds the fountains and springs). And this river, which afterwards goes to water the Sultan's orange-trees, so often, thanks to these women, carries dead bodies with it, that it has been found necessary to bar it with an iron grating before it reaches the gardens.

It seems that the irresistible way—and, moreover, the traditional, almost obligatory way—to ingratiate oneself with a fair divorcée is to take her a sugar-loaf. (The men and women of Morocco have a surprisingly sweet tooth.)

When, therefore, at the close of day, you perceive a mysterious gentleman passing along the walls, smuggling a sugar-loaf in his burnous, you are not likely to be wrong if you doubt the purity of his intentions.

Who would believe, on a first view, that such a town could contain little things so pitiful and comical ?

CHAPTER XXVI

22nd April.

WE are invited to luncheon at the house of the Vizier of War, Si Mohammed-ben-el-Arbi.

It has rained in torrents throughout the night. It rains still as we file laboriously, on horseback, through the narrow little streets, grazing the walls with our knees and jostling the grey-hooded passers-by into the doorways. In the thousand turnings of the labyrinth, which has resumed its piteous air of rainy days, we march for half-an-hour, escorted by soldiers, and obliged sometimes to bend completely over our horses' necks in the darkness of the low vaults. Once again, we send in spurts all about us the fetid, sticky mud, which re-forms immediately at Fez with every shower.

We dismount in the middle of a pool, in front of a miserable little narrow doorway which is the entrance of this vizier. The first passages of his house, paved in white and green mosaics, follow one another in maze-like turnings, in order that the eyes of passers-by may not penetrate into the interior. But at the end is

a larger door, opening on to something
unexpected and magnificent : a large, majestic
court ; festooned porticoes, with sculptures
enhanced by colours and gold ; a strange,
slow, religious music, played and sung by an
invisible orchestra and choir; men in costumes
of fairyland, advancing towards us over a
marble floor.

When the Alhambra was inhabited and bright
with gold and living, there were enacted there,
I imagine, such scenes as this. Perhaps the
colours here, the reds and blues and golds,
are a little too vivid, for the house, strangely
enough, is new ; but the total effect is one
of harmony for all that. I have seen similar
settings, similar costumes, in a theatre; what
is astonishing is that such things should still
exist in reality.

The court is rectangular and very large ; it is
bordered by high walls of immaculate whiteness,
which are crowned, all around, by a frieze of
blue and pink arabesques and a row of tiles
in green faience ; in the centre a fountain
springs from a round basin and breaks into a
little cascade, mingling its sound with that of
the invisible and solemn music.

On the two long sides of the quadrilateral
stretch cornices of cedarwood, in broad pro-
jection from the walls ; painted in a brilliant red

N

that stands out vividly against the whiteness of the walls, they are ornamented with large geometrical roses of blue and gold, in an extraordinary complication. They overhang a series of ogival doorways masked on the inside by hanging muslins; and behind these veils we can hear the whispering of the hidden women who are watching us.

In the middle of each of the two shorter sides of the quadrilateral, those naturally which are farthest from each other, are monumental doorways that are marvels of design and colour. The first arch is festooned with stalactites of snowy whiteness, which seem to hang in clusters, to be superposed and intermixed like the fantasies of hoarfrost. Above these long white drops is a second ogival arch, set off with blue and red and gold. And above again is built up an indescribable crowning, reaching almost to the top of the wall. It is composed of delicate polychromatic arabesques, interwoven with gold; it is a scaffolding of that rare lace-work such as formerly was worked at Granada in rose-coloured stucco, on the walls of the Alhambra. The two folds of these doors are thrown wide open; they are entirely carved, painted and gilt, in kaleidoscopic roses; their predominant colour is a metallic green, and they resemble the outspread tails of peacocks.

These two monumental entrances face each other at opposite ends of the court; they have long curtains half of blue and half of gooseberry-coloured cloth embroidered with gold, against which stand out, whiter yet, the denticulations of their stalactites. And these curtains, drawn back, disclose in the interior the usual luxury of carpets and cushions and gold-embroidered silks.

Amongst the persons who come before us, there is first the Vizier of War, headed like an Egyptian sphinx, with the principal chiefs of the army. Behind them follow negro and negress slaves, adorned with necklaces, and gewgaws, and large metal rings. All these people, in slippers, glide noiselessly over the gleaming marble, to the sound of the slow, rhythmic music accompanied now by iron castanets.

Passing under the stalactites of the door at the farther end, we enter with our hosts an apartment furnished in European style, but furnished very strangely: four-post beds, draped in rose-coloured and peacock-blue brocades; gilt arm-chairs, upholstered in figured tapestry; on the walls whitewash and arabesques; and, on silver dishes placed on the floor, Spanish coffers, in the form of Gothic shrines, filled with sweetmeats.

The music is quite near us, in an adjoining room. The choir sings in falsetto, very high as always; it reminds one of some religious Office in the Sistine Chapel; and the orchestra, of strings, gives out a potent sound. The same movements recur unceasingly, renewed with a kind of graduated and growing exaltation.

Amongst the tall, white-robed Arabs is an extraordinary little being, clothed in a rich assortment of colours, who is the recipient of much adulation. 'Tis a child of seven or eight years, the favourite son of the vizier, born of one of his black slaves. (In Morocco, these children have the same standing in the family as those of the white wives; it is one of the causes of the degeneracy of the Arab race, which is becoming more and more infiltrated with Nubian blood.) He wears a jonquil robe, veiled by a surplice of white net; a pale-blue burnous; a broad riband of mignonette-green silk sustaining a little Koran in a kind of satchel; and orange slippers embroidered with violet and gold. He has a charming, comical little face, half Arab, half negro; on the almost blue-white of his wide-open eyes his dancing pupils roll rapidly, constantly.

In the next room are the musicians, to the number of forty, all in their state burnouses, of different colours, and sitting in circle on the floor on cushions. Each of them plays and sings at one and the same time, in a kind of delirium, the head thrown back, the mouth wide open. Some have large mandolines of inlaid work, the strings of which they touch with pieces of wood. Others have violins completely encrusted with mother-of-pearl. They play them with very large curved bows, which are ornamented with designs in mother-of-pearl and ebony, imitating the scales on the skins of snakes. The violins are in the form of large clogs, with ends turned up after the manner of a ship's prow.

The luncheon is laid in the apartment opposite to that in which we were received, behind the other festoon of stalactites, at the other extremity of the court, which we have to cross again in the brilliant sunshine.

It is served somewhat after the European manner; the interdicted wine being replaced by tea, which servants prepare as required in tall silver samovars. The plates and dishes are Japanese; the glasses are gilt and variegated with colours; and all this, which, at home, would, in its total effect, seem loud and vulgar, is here in perfect harmony with the splendour of the surrounding colours.

There are something like twenty-two courses. The black slaves, busy, distracted, cross the court in all directions. The dishes are so copious that a single man has difficulty in holding them; there are quarters of sheep, pyramids of chickens, mountains of fish, couscous as for an ogre's feast. To these are added other edibles, under the large, inevitable cones of white esparto ornamented with red designs; and all these cones accumulate on the ground, forming in the court a kind of depot of gigantic Chinese hats. The music continues to play during the long feast. While the luncheon proceeds we watch continuously, through the denticulated door, the beautiful marble court, its fountains, its whiteness, its multi-coloured arabesques, and as we watch the summit of the walls is gradually crowned with women's heads, curious to catch a glimpse of us even from afar. They are behind, no doubt, on their terrace promenade; we see pass only their tiara-like head-dresses, their foreheads and the shaded lines of their eyes; they look like great cats on the prowl. And they follow one another in a never-ending train.

CHAPTER XXVII

23rd April.

RUMOUR has it that the *Sultan of the Tholbas* is in flight since last night.

He was an ephemeral king, a little outside the walls, in his improvised, white canvas town. At the door of his tent he had a counterfeit battery of large cannons, made of pieces of wood and reeds. He was, though with more dignity, something like the " Pope of Fools " of our Middle Ages.

In the university of Fez, which has remained unchanged since the epoch of Arab splendour, it is an ancient custom, each year, in the spring vacation, for the students to spend ten days in high festival; to choose a king (who buys his election, at auction, by force of gold); to encamp with him in the fields on the river bank; then to levy a tax upon the population of the town, in order to be able at night to make merry with song and music, couscous and cups of tea. And the people of the town lend themselves to these amusements with a smiling submission; they come, all— viziers, merchants, craftsmen, by corporations and with banners at their head—to visit the camp of the *tholbas* and bring presents. And, finally, about the eighth day, the Sultan himself, the true Sultan, comes also to pay homage to the Sultan of the Students, who receives him on horseback, under a parasol like a caliph, and treats him as an equal, calling him "my brother."

The *Sultan of the Tholbas* is always a member of one of the distant tribes, who has some special favour to ask for himself or for his people, and he profits by this unique interview with the sovereign to obtain it. Very soon afterwards, for fear lest it should be taken from him, for fear also of reprisals on the part of those whom he has had to punish in the cause of good government, one fine night, clandestinely, he disappears—an easy thing to do in Morocco; across the deserted campaign he seeks refuge in his own country.

At the end of these days of mirth the students re-enter into Fez. Those of them who have not completed their studies return to their little work-cells, in those kinas of cloisters, strangely poor-looking, that are called *mederças* and are places almost holy, forbidden to unbelievers. The Sultan sends daily to each of them a loaf of bread, which constitutes almost the whole of their usual fare; others also receive hospitality from individuals in the town; it is counted highly meritorious for a family to lodge and board a *tholba*. During the day they live in the mosques, especially in the immense Karaouin, squatted down to listen to the lectures of the learned professors, or kneeling in the act of prayer. Those who, after seven or eight years of study, have obtained their degree of doctor and marabout return to their own country surrounded with a high prestige. As I have said, they have come sometimes from very distant parts, these *tholbas* of Karaouin; they have gathered from the four winds of Islam, attracted by the renown of this holy mosque, which contains, it seems, in its libraries, ageless and priceless volumes, accumulated there in the days of Arab greatness, brought from Alexandria or carried off from the convents of Spain. And when they return to the distant countries from which they had set out, they have become priests apt to preach a religious war; they have " plucked a rose " in the impenetrable mosque. It is Karaouin which gives the fierce signal to the whole of Mussulman Africa; and Karaouin lies in Al Moghreb like a centre of immobility and sleep.

The sciences taught at Karaouin include astrology, alchemy and divination. The " mystic numbers " are studied there, and the influence of the stars and of demons, and other tenebrous things which for the moment have disappeared from the rest of the world—until the day perhaps when, in another form, shorn of the marvellous, they will reappear triumphant as the beyond of our positive sciences. The Koran and all its commentators are paraphrased at great length, as also Aristotle and other ancient philosophers. And side by side with so many grave and arid things, extraordinary affectations of style, of diction, of grammar, subtleties of the Middle Ages which we are no longer able to understand; they are like the designs, so elaborate, so delicate, wrought here and there on the grim bastions and the high walls.

And since I have spoken of these super-annuated elegances, I will quote the opening of a reply of a vizier, an old student of Karaouin, to a foreign diplomat:

" We have brought your letter to the know-ledge of our illustrious master (whom God render victorious). In reading it we have made ourselves the interpreter of your senti-ments, accentuating your words with art, for the persuasiveness of a good diction is sweeter than the purest of water, more subtle than the most delicate of love potions. Dictated by the kindliest sentiments, your letter seemed to us as pleasant as a cool breeze," etc., etc.

CHAPTER XXVIII

24th April.

IN the bright hours of the morning, walking on my terraces—which are in compartments, in little staged platforms—I discover a new dependency of this domain of roofs, communicating with the part already known by a stretch of wall which up till now it had not occurred to me to overpass. It is a new little square promenade admirably placed so as to be in shadow during the early hours of the day, while the other serves so excellently for watching the setting of the sun on the vanishing distances of the outspread town.

From this observatory I have quite a different view. First of all, indiscreet glimpses on to adjacent houses overtopping mine and rearing their terraces and stretches of wall against the blue sky; as it is morning the housekeepers have, according to custom, spread out on lines, in the sunshine and pure air, the striped bedclothes, the motley-coloured cushions, all the various kinds of articles of bedding that have served during the night, and their vivid colours shine out against the cracked greyness of the walls. And above these things a distant palm-tree shows the little bunch of plumes at its top; and higher still climbs a fragment of a mountain blue with aloes, and dotted with tombs and ruins and the *koubas* of holy personages defunct, quite a little cemetery perched above the town. I stroll about and look around. And, suddenly, behind a little wall, not more than two paces from me, I see a piece of gilt finery shining. As I watch it moves, then mounts slowly, slowly, with infinite precautions : a woman's *hantouze* ! (One of my neighbours, evidently, who has heard footsteps and is curious to know to whom they can belong.) I stand quite still, suddenly turned to stone. The gilt head-dress continues to ascend ; presently emerges a head-band of sequins ; then hair—a forehead—two black eyebrows, two large eyes which have seen me ! Fool ! It is finished. . . . Disappeared, my beauty—like a puppet in a Punch and Judy show.

I wait, nevertheless, divining well that she has not gone. And in fact, here again comes the *hantouze,* mounting, mounting ; then the whole face appears, this time, and regards me boldly, with a half smile of scandalised curiosity. She is charming, this neighbour of mine, seen thus mysteriously, in her golden head-dress on this background of ruins. But truly we are too

near one another, and I do wrong to remain ;
I feel myself that I am an intruder, and in order
not to prolong this first presentation I with-
draw to my lower terrace—where I have other
neighbours already more accustomed to me.

Here, indeed, it is much less intimate ; in
place of that uprearing of houses surmounted
by a distant cemetery, I have below my feet
the whole panorama of Fez, with its gardens, its
walls, and the snow-capped Atlas in the background of the picture ; it is an immense and
complete setting, and my indiscretion here, being
less particularised, seems to me more admissible.
Generally, when I appear, the little walls all
round about are adorned with the heads of
women, always idle and curious to examine the
rare kind of neighbour that I am for them.
The air of startled gazelles, the shyness of the
first days, have quickly disappeared. What
would be an enormity of imprudence with a
Mussulman seems free from danger with me
who will tell no one, and who, besides, am soon
to depart for my fantastic country so far, so
very far away. What is essential is that the
husbands should know nothing of it. And they
look at me, they smile at me, they make signs
of greeting to me. They even come and show me,
from a little distance, various objects, to know
what I think of them, ornaments for the arms and

breast, golden nets for covering the *hantouzes*. My gloves are a source of extreme astonishment: "Oh! have you seen?" they say. "He has hands with two skins!" I dwell in a rich neighbourhood, and thus all these women have nothing to do from morning till evening but take turns in entertaining their spouse.

One of them, who belongs to one of the richest of my neighbours, moves about like a captive beast. She spends hours alone, seated in equilibrium on the narrow summit of a wall, outlined against the sky; motionless and indifferent to everything, even to the curiosity of seeing me. Not absolutely pretty, especially on a first impression, but lissom and admirably modelled, young and strange, with shadowed eyes, which one divines are darkly circled by some unrestful weariness. She is at her post this morning, arms bare, legs crossed and bare also to the knees; on her ankles, delicately slim, weigh coarse, heavy rings, and a pair of old, nondescript slippers hang loosely on her small and shapely feet. Her eyes are heavier than usual, and she looks as if she had been weeping. I am sure that it is she who was whipped last night. I heard the blows through my wall, and for an hour afterwards the sound of weeping, and cries of rage.

Then I perceive a new figure, a tall, dusky girl,

half-child, half-woman, bare-headed, with long
tresses of beautiful hair. Whence comes this
recruit ? Who is the rich neighbour that has
bought her ardent youth, her superb body ?
A profile straight and firm ; eyes very elongated,
scarcely open, dark and sensuous ; an air at
once haughty and shy ; her arm, which is bare,
would in itself be a marvellous thing to carve
or paint. After a minute of timidity, she, too,
like the others, ends by looking me full in the
face, as who should say : " What are you doing
there ? Why do you come thus to annoy the
women in their domain of roofs ? "

And I turn away and look at the other, the
solitary, who preserves still an air of wayward-
ness and revolt on her edge of wall.

Decidedly, she has, at first sight, that kind
of irregularity of feature, almost of plainness,
which sometimes ends, on longer acquaintance,
in becoming for us the supreme charm. She
has lips of firm and delicate contour, deeply
dimpled at the corners, such as often constitute
the whole attractive and mortal beauty of a
woman's face. And the idea that she has been
beaten, and will be beaten again, is extremely
painful to me this morning. I long to be able to
prevent her tears and suffering ; to bring her a
little physical ease, a little rest.

I make no merit of this kind of pity ; rather

am I confounded by it, for I know perfectly well that I should be less concerned about her and her grief if it were not for that delicious mouth of hers.

The all-powerful influence of external charm works upon those of our sentiments which ought to be the freest from it—so that one can be kind or less kind to one creature or another, according to her outward form and favour.

.　　.　　.　　.　　.　　.　　.

Ten o'clock, the hour to dress for luncheon with the Minister, at the embassy. And it is one of my amusements to present myself in Arab costume. There, in the alleys of the garden of orange-trees or in the court of denticulated arches, 'tis a pleasing thing to flaunt burnous and caftan over the pavements of painted tiles, and to imagine for the moment that one is a personage of Alhambra.

The sun has dried the mud of the town and brightened the colours of the old walls ; in the darkness of the little streets, magnificent long rays fall here and there on passing veils and burnouses.

Preceded by one or two domestics, as befits a man of condition, I issue from my house with the grave leisureliness that becomes the place in which I am, the costume I have adopted. When I have drawn to, behind me, by its heavy

knocker, my diminutive door studded and overlaid with iron, I turn, in the rusty, centuries-old
lock, a key that weighs three pounds. Then I
set out, first along narrow, covered passages,
which seem rather outer corridors than streets;
and yet somehow, from the strange transparency
of the gloom that reigns there, one divines that
outside, where the sky appears, there exists a
calm splendour of light. I meet two or three
pedestrians walking like me in bare feet, noiselessly; at the moment when we pass we each
flatten ourselves against the wall, effacing our
shoulders, and nevertheless our veils brush.
Twice I turn to the right; I cross a little bazaar
of fruits and vegetables, also covered; then
turning to the left I reach a wider street—in the
open air, this one—where I behold at last the
incomparable blue, between two rows of old
white walls which are the walls of mosques;
the sunny side is dazzling, the shady side bluish
and almost ash-coloured. A little neglected and
ruinous both of them, the mosque on the right
and the mosque on the left; but in the old walls,
shapeless under repeated replasterings and coats
of whitewash, their doors are still intact and
exquisite; they have kept their framings of
mosaics; their roses, now strangely complicated,
now quite simple, like large full-blown daisies;
their rows of starry designs, the thousand

o

painted facets of which sparkle with colour, very old, and nevertheless very fresh.

Some yards farther on, the wall in shadow breaks from top to base, then ends, completely overthrown, disclosing a holy courtyard where venerated dead sleep beneath mosaic flagstones overgrown with weeds and wild poppies. And here, too, as we pass, we have to turn obliquely from the sunny side to avoid a stork that is busy putting its home to rights, in an immense nest on the edge of a tiny minaret, and scatters on to the street below blades of dried grass and fragments of plaster. And the sunshine, and the immobility, and the mystery, and the charm of all this, how shall one tell it!

It is this corner, perhaps, now so familiar, which will remain the longest graven in my memory. Why, I may never be able to explain. I know not how it is that I feel such an enchantment as I pass, each day, along this street, between these old mosques, in the yet matutinal sunshine. I experience a kind of artist's joy in representing to myself how remote and inaccessible the place is, how little ordinary, and in adding to it by my presence one detail more, which a painter would not fail to note. I think it is above all for the pleasure of passing there and of taking myself seriously in these vizier's robes that I have these changing fancies for a golden caftan or a pale blue caftan, veiled under white draperies and girt by silken cords of rarest colours. I endeavour to look as natural as may be in these costumes, so as not to attract the notice of passers-by, and yesterday some Berber mountaineers, taking me for a chief of the town, transported me to the seventh heaven by saluting me in Arab fashion. There is a large dose of childishness in my composition, I am forced to recognise it. But to those who shrug their shoulders, I avow that this whimsey of mine does not seem sensibly more foolish than to pass the evening at a club, to read the election addresses of candidates for Parliament, or to delight in the perfect fit and fashion of an English jacket, or a fancy waistcoat.

Leaving this chosen street by a turning on the right and passing through other narrow passages I quickly arrive at the Minister's house. There, as soon as I cross the threshold, I am in the midst of guards, always the same ; in the midst of kaids, of cavaliers who have followed us from Tangier and have pitched their tents amongst the flowering rose-trees of the garden, under the orange-trees and under the clear blue sky— persons all well known, who come towards me smiling. They arrange a fold here and there of my *haik*, of my burnous, and try to initiate me into the refinement of Arab fashion, greatly

pleased that I should array myself as one of
them. " It is much more becoming, isn't it ? "
they say. (Oh yes, beyond a doubt.) And
they add: " If you dress like this when you
return to your own country, everyone will want
to wear the Moroccan costume." (But that—
no, I think not; I cannot well imagine this
fashion becoming general on the boulevards.)

After the delightful garden follows a corridor
where, immediately on entering, I hear the
sound of running water; and ultimately I
reach the large interior two-staged court, which
is the marvel of the dwelling; a pavement of
mosaics, in which the thousand little designs
in blue and yellow, white and black, glisten with
a moistened brightness; all around, a series
of Moorish arcades with denticulated festoons,
and, on the upper stage, above these arches and
arabesques of stone, an open-work gallery of
cedarwood.

The water springs from a white marble basin
in the centre and also from an exquisite mural
fountain set in one of the walls. This fountain
is a kind of large ogive of mosaics in which are
intermixed starry designs of most admirable
form; a band of black and white tiles frames
all this embroidery of multi-coloured roses, and
above, by way of crowning, hang pendentives
of snowy whiteness, like the stalactites of a cave.

The rooms open on to this court by immense cedar doors; within, the walls are decorated, up to half their height, by blue and red velvet hangings with embroideries of gold imitating large arches.

.   .   .   .

There I find the Minister with all the other companions of our journey, and, at his table, served in European fashion, a little of the genial merriment which used to characterise our meals in the tent. For a moment I put foot again in the modern world; this palace (which belongs to a vizier who has been dislodged for our convenience) seems to have become a little corner of France.

.   .   .   .

The hour of coffee and the cigarette of the East follows; an hour passed in the shadows of a colonnaded verandah, before the old, old kiosk of the garden, buried under coats of whitewash. From here, one has a view of the tranquil little grove of orange-trees surrounded by high walls, and encumbered, amongst the brushwood and the roses, by Bedouin tents.

CHAPTER XXIX

25th April.

I ALMOST feel that I will write no more, finding more and more ordinary the things that surround me.

When I go out, it seems to me quite natural to descend my dark staircase, to find outside my door my mule, ordered in advance, awaiting me with its high-peaked saddle, to mount from the very threshold of my house, for fear of soiling my long white draperies and my slippers in the mud of out of doors ; and to set off at random through the dark, narrow little streets.

It matters not whither I go, to spots deserted or amongst the crowds, to the bazaar or into the fields.

Oh ! the murmur of this bazaar, the silent movement of these burnouses, in the confused half-gloom ! In and out in a maze go the little avenues, covered with old roofings of wood, or else with trellis-work of reeds entwined with vine branches. And all their length is lined by little shops, scarcely larger than kennels, in which squat the turbaned shopkeepers, impassive and superb in the midst of their rare toys.

It is in quarters, in rows, that the shops of the same kind are grouped. There is the street of the merchants of clothes, where the stalls gleam with silks of divers colours, rose, blue, orange and nasturtium, with broideries of silver and gold, and it is there the white women linger, veiled and draped like phantoms. There is the street of the leather merchants, where hang thousands of multi-coloured trappings for horses, mules and asses; all kinds of accessories of hunt and war, in strange and ancient shapes, powder-horns spangled with silver and brass, embroidered straps for gun and sabre, travelling bags for caravans, and amulets for crossing the desert.

Then the streets of the brass merchants, where, from morning till evening, one hears the arabesques being hammered on tray and vase. The streets of the embroiderers of slippers, where all the little kennels are filled with velvet, with beads and gold. The street of the painters of whatnots; that of the smiths, naked and black; that of the dyers, their arms stained with indigo and purple. Finally, the quarter of the gunsmiths, the makers of the long, flint-locks, slender as reeds, the stocks of which are encrusted with silver and enlarged so as to grip the shoulder. (The Moroccans never think of modifying this fashion adopted by their

ancestors; the form of the guns, like all else in
this country, is immutable; and one imagines
one is dreaming in seeing the manufacture in
such quantities of these arms of olden times.

It swarms and murmurs confusedly, the crowd
clothed in grey wool, which has come from afar
to buy and sell extraordinary little things.
Sorcerers make their incantations, armed bands
pass, dancing a war dance and firing their
guns, to the sound of mournful bagpipes and
tabours; beggars show their sores; negro slaves
shoulder their loads; asses roll themselves in
the dust. The ground, of the same grey colour
as the crowd, is littered with refuse, with the
excrement of animals, the feathers of fowls,
with dead mice; and everyone, in trailing
slippers, treads the filth underfoot.

How far away this life is from ours! The
activity of this people is as strange to us as its
immobility and its sleep. With the movement
of this burnoused crowd there is yet mingled
an indefinable detachment, a supreme indifference, such as amongst us is unknown. The
hooded heads of the men, the veiled heads of
the women, pursue, in the midst of their traffick-
ing, the same religious dream; five times a day
they turn to prayer, and ponder above all else
eternity and death. Amongst the crowd are
sordid beggars with the eyes of visionaries; and

men in filthy rags whose movements are noble
and their faces the faces of prophets.

"*Balaak! Balaak!*" that is the eternal cry
of Arab crowds. ("*Balaak!*" means something
like " Make way ! ")

"*Balaak!*" When the little asses pass, in long
lines, laden with bales so large that they knock
against the pedestrians and overthrow them.
"*Balaak!*" for the slow-moving camels, that
rock to the sound of their little bells. "*Balaak!*"
for the handsome horses of the kaids, harnessed
in marvellous colours, that gallop and rear.
One never returns from this bazaar without
having been jostled by someone or something,
charged by a horse or soiled by a dust-covered
donkey—"*Balaak!*"

People of every tribe come and go and
congregate ; negroes from the Soudan, and
fair-skinned Arabs ; autochthonous Berbers,
Mussulmans without conviction, whose women
are veiled only from the mouth ; green-
turbaned erkwas, unrelenting fanatics, who
turn their heads and spit at sight of a Christian.
Every day one encounters the " saint," uttering
her prophecies at the crossways. And the
" saint " her male counterpart, an old man,
absolutely naked, with not so much as a girdle,
who walks and walks, with never a stop, like
the Wandering Jew, very rapidly through the

crowds, in a perpetual haste, muttering his prayers. At intervals is a little corner open to the sky, a little square, where grows perhaps a green mulberry-tree or the enormous trunk of a centuries-old vine with twisted branches like a sheaf of serpents. And then, one passes the *fondaks*, which are kinds of caravanserais for foreign traders : large many-staged courtyards surrounded with colonnades and open-work galleries of cedarwood, and devoted each to a special kind of merchandise. There is the *fondak* of the traders in tea and Indian wood ; that of the traders in carpets from the western provinces ; that of spices and that of silks ; that of slaves and that of salt.

All this part of the bazaar is reputed hardly safe for us ; it is considered holy ground, on account of the mosques of Karaouin and Mulai-Edriss, which are contained within it. And, at the approaches to Mulai-Edriss, the smaller but more sacred of the two, the streets are barred to the height of one's middle by huge pieces of wood, such as are placed in fields to enclose cattle. We must beware of crossing them, at risk of our life ; the approaches to this mosque, as venerable in Islam as the Kasbah of Mecca, must never be defiled by the foot of a Christian, or of a Jew.

At the entrance to the bazaar I have a

chosen corner where, each day, I leave my mule in charge of one of my servants, so that I may know where to find it on my return, when my purchases are done.

And it is especially at the departure, at the issue from the darksome labyrinth, that the place of which I speak seems a luminous setting of "The Thousand and One Nights." Then, suddenly, the dark and narrow street expands; expands fanwise, forming a triangular open space on which a ray of sunshine falls from a patch of blue sky. The background of this little space—where many other saddled mules are waiting, like mine, at the foot of a century-old vine—is ornamented in its middle by a gushing fountain: a mosaic arch, set in the side wall of a projecting house, from which two jets of water issue to fall into a marble basin—all this so ancient, so shapeless, so dilapidated, that there are no words in which to express such aspects of antiquity. On the right of the fountain a little street paved in breakneck fashion ascends a steep slope and buries itself in darkness, under a broken and sinister vault. (It is by this street that presently we shall have to disappear, my mule and I, on the way back to our lodging in the upper part of Old Fez.) On the left is an inimitable monumental gateway, more beautiful than any in the town, than any gate of the mosques—and nevertheless leading nowhither, only into a mournful courtyard. It is an immense ogive, garlanded with the rarest arabesques, the most exquisite mosaics. Above this entrance stretches a large horizontal band of religious inscriptions, in faience, black letters on a white ground. Above that again, a row of little aligned ogives, filled each with a different kind of arabesque, with carvings like embroidery, like lace—some with very large designs, alternating with others with very small designs, in such a way as to accentuate still more the ingenious variety of the ornamentation.

And, higher still, an indescribable crowning of stalactites juts out, forming as it were a very salient lintel, a kind of cornice. All these stalactites, absolutely regular and geometrical, are compacted with another, cover one another, are superposed in masses one upon another, with an extreme complication. In places they resemble the thousands of compartments of a beehive; elsewhere, higher up, the little droppings of hoarfrost. And all these so laboriously fashioned things form in their entirety series of marvellously festooned arches of an exquisite curve. A layer of earthy dust dims the colours of the faience; all the delicate carvings are chipped, blackish, entangled with the webs of spiders and the nests of birds. And this gateway of fairyland gives, needless to say, an impression of extreme antiquity, as likewise this fountain, this little open space, this pavement, these tottering houses; as likewise this whole town, this whole people. Indeed, the art of the Arabs is so associated in my mind with ideas of dust and death that I can scarcely imagine it in days when it was young, and all its colours fresh.

Outside the bazaar, the labyrinth of Fez becomes darker and more deserted; few of the byways are open to the air; the vine-bowers and straw roofs are replaced by ceilings óf wood or by ogives of masonry, which every two yards or so cross the street, surmounted by expanses of wall as high as the house-tops, and as mournful and blank as the houses themselves. It is as if one were travelling at the bottom of a series of wells communicating with one another by arches; only in snatches does one see the blue or the grey of the sky; and it is almost impossible to find one's way in the inextricable network. There again, by the side of quarters empty and dead, there are crowds; there, again, the "*Balaak!*" is to be heard. "*Balaak!*" for grave and thoughtful men who are leaving a mosque after the prayer. "*Balaak!*" for restive mules which have butressed themselves sideways, refusing to go either forward or back. "*Balaak!*" for herds of oxen, which come trotting in line, their horns low and threatening, along little dark passages that are scarcely large enough for their great bodies.

CHAPTER XXX

26th April.

AFTER the first hours of sleep in my solitary dwelling, I perceive a ray of moonlight that comes to me freely from the sky, between the disjointed folds of my cedar door. Then in the distance of the resonant night, I hear a psalmody of high-pitched, mournful voices droning their cries of ardent faith, their chanted plaints which seem the expression of all our terrestrial nothingness. It is two o'clock in the morning, the hour of the first prayer of this new day, which soon the eternal sun will come to enlighten. It is like an immense canticle to Allah, a dream canticle sometimes exalted, sometimes slow and plaintive; and mournful always, so mournful that it makes one shudder, for the muezzins, like the Arab bagpipes, have borrowed from the jackals something of the timbre of their voices.

For a long time this sing-song hovers over the grey tranquillity of the sleeping town. Then silence returns, dead silence.

The last hours of the night ebb away. In the fresh calm of the very early morning, at the break of day, mingled with the crowing of cocks, the voices of these men recommence their psalmody, in a growing exaltation of prayer; it is five o'clock, the hour of to-day's second Office; the hour, too, when the Sultan priest, clothed all in white, rises in his palace to begin his austere, religious day.

Then the booming of a distant cannon announces the day, the holy day of Friday; then arises a general hymn, then the bagpipes begin to wail, the drums to roll. The night is ended and the sun is risen.

.　　.　　.　　.　　.　　.　　.

Alone, early in the morning, dressed as an Arab, and on foot—although this is a very undignified thing to do—I set off for the bazaar to buy some rose-water and scented Indian wood, in order that I may perfume my house in the customary manner. And never have I felt so completely as this morning the gratifying illusion of being an inhabitant of Fez.

The bazaar, which has only just opened its thousand little shops, is still tranquil and almost deserted. The rush lattice-work and tender new leaves of the vine branches, which roof it an interminable succession of arbours, filter the morning sunshine, sift a bright and joyous light. The perfumes for which I have come are sold in the same quarter as unwoven silks and beads. And this quarter is the most coloured in the bazaar—in the strict sense of the word colour. In long and narrow perspective, through a succession of little streets, hang thousands of things in line on the raised shutters of the niches, blotting out the merchants who sit cross-legged within : they are skeins without number of silk and skeins of golden thread ; they are masses of gilt beads and pink beads ; and of those tasselled cords (to hold suspended from men's necks the sabres and holy books), which, as I have said, are one of the chief adorn- ments of the Arab costume. And a number of persons, very dignified and very handsome in their white monkish hoods, move noiselessly about in slippers, choosing from amongst the hanging girdles the particular colour that will harmonise best with a particular costume.

And here, before a toy shop, is an old woman, veiled like a phantom, but with kindly eyes, buying a comical little doll for her grand- daughter, a mite of three or four years, an adorable little thing with eyes like those of an Angora kitten, and hair and nails already tinted with red henna. This morning all this appears before me under an exterior of tran- quillity and simple good nature. And all the mystery too, all the gloom, which at first sight seem to envelop things, disappear very quickly

P

as we become more familiar with their aspect. I know now every corner of the bazaar, and certain of the merchants, when I pass, give me good-day, invite me to sit down.

Involuntarily my steps always lead me back to the dark little streets that circle Karaouin. There, too, the mystery has disappeared and the impression of the first day, so strange, so startling, is not to be recaptured. I stand before its gateways, gazing long into the interior; very little would make me enter; I find it difficult to imagine that to do so would probably cost me my life. It would seem to me quite natural to go and kneel beside these people, whose clothes I wear.

Very varied are the aspects of Karaouin, changing with the different gateways through which one gazes. I do not wonder that at first sight we could distinguish nothing of its general plan. It is a kind of accumulation of mosques, of different epochs and different styles. It is a town of columns and arches of every Arab form—sometimes heavy arches, crushing squat pillars, which follow one another in endless perspectives, with innumerable lamps suspended in the darkness of the ceilings; sometimes courts, inundated with sunshine and vaulted by the blue sky, surrounded by tall slender columns and infinitely denticulated

arches of a design always rare and exquisite.
And never has Karaouin been so beautiful as
to-day, in this dazzling sunshine, which radiates
and penetrates everywhere, clear and white,
making the marbles gleam, and the mosaics
without end, and the water of the gushing
fountains.

One of the gateways, in the shadow of which
I pause for preference, opens on to the largest
and most wonderful of the courts, paved with
faience and marble. On the sides are little
projecting kiosks—rather are they little
dais—like, but more beautiful than, those
of the celebrated "Court of Lions" in the
Alhambra; there are the same groupings of
columns, supporting indescribable open-work
arcades that seem to have been made by a
patient superposition of pendants of rime—
the whole set off with a little gold, dying under
the dust of centuries, and a little blue, a little
pink, with I know not what other pale colours.
And, on the uprights, quite straight and flat
and designedly rigid, which separate these
festooned porticoes, layers of carvings, inimitable in delicacy and design, are outspread and
intertwined, graven to different depths; it is as
if old, fairy gossamers had been hung there in
many thicknesses one above another.

And light, light as air, seem all these kiosks,

light as little castles that one might build for sylphs in the clouds with the crystal facets of hail and snow. And, at the same time, the rigid straightness of the great lines, the employment solely of geometrical combinations, the absence of every form inspired by nature, by man or beast, give to the whole an air of austere purity, of something immaterial, religious.

The sunshine floods this court; all the mosaics, all the tiles gleam with a pearly lustre. The jet of rippling water that plays from the fountain in the middle has changing colours of opal or of rainbow, and stands out against the exquisitely intricate background of a large interior door, which, like the kiosks of the sides, is in filigree-work of Alhambra. And, as it is Friday, quite a crowd of white burnouses is prostrated on the flagstones in motionless prayer.

From the darkness outside, from the kind of night that fills this skirting road where I am obliged to remain hidden, in doubtful security— all these forbidden things assume in my eyes an air of enchantment.

.   .   .   .

The " saint " is infatuated with me this morning. Clothed in rags of orange-coloured silk, her cheeks vermilioned, her eyes dilated and

wild, she follows me obstinately to the exit of
the bazaar, uttering in a high voice incomprehensible things that seem to me almost like
benedictions. Evidently she has been misled
by my movements and costume. And un-
comfortable at feeling her behind me, I throw
her some pieces of money in order that she
may let me go my way in peace.

.   .   .   .

An hour later in the market-place—the
clamorous hour, the hour of business and of
multitude.

About this large open space, which is a kind
of rectangular plain, move burnouses and veils,
the whole hooded and masked crowd, whitish
and grey, to which here and there the shepherds
in their camel-hair *sayons* add spots of yellowish-
brown, and the donkeys spots of reddish-brown.
Hundreds of women are seated on the ground,
selling bread, and butter, and vegetables, their
faces invisible, enveloped in muslin. And in
the background of this place, and this crowd,
rise the high walls of Fez, gloomy and gigantic,
dwarfing everything, the points of their battlements outlined against the sky. Needless to
say one hears the tabours and the bagpipes.
Here and there the pointed hoods congregate
and make a compact circle around captivating
spectacles: there are snake - charmers; there

are men who stick pins into their tongues;
those who hack their scalps ; those who remove
an eyeball from its socket with a wooden pallet
and deposit it on their cheek ; all gipsydom and
all vagrancy. To me, who am leaving the day
after to-morrow, these now familiar things will
seem very astonishing when I have returned
to our modern world, and recall them from a
distance. For the moment I belong in all
verity to a past epoch, and I mingle with all the
naturalness in the world in this life here, which
is similar in all respects, I imagine, to the life
of the popular quarters of Granada or Cordova
in the times of the Moors.

To-morrow is my last day. I am leaving
behind me at Fez the embassy, which is detained
by the slowness of things political, and shall
depart alone, with Captain H. de V***, in a
little private caravan. It should be very
interesting, and perhaps a little adventurous.
We are going to Mekinez, the other holy town,
more dilapidated and dead even than Fez ; and
from there to faithless Tangier, where, suddenly,
our dream of Islam and ancient days will end.
I have not had time to become attached to my
little Mussulman dwelling here, and now I must
leave it and forget it, as I have forgotten already
so many other foreign dwellings scattered
everywhere about the earth. Yet would I

willingly have lingered there for a week or two longer. With a few mats, a few old hangings and arms, it had quickly become very habitable, all without losing its little airs of mystery, its difficult approaches.

CHAPTER XXXI

27th April.

WE are invited to luncheon with the Kaid El-Meshwar (the introducer of ambassadors). And we repair to his house on horseback, preceded by his guards, large-turbaned and armed with huge sticks, whom he has sent to meet us at our very door.

The great court of his house is even more beautiful than that of the Vizier of War. It is above all more ancient, and the years, the centuries, have dimmed, with their inimitable effacement, the colours and the golds.

Rows of interior porticoes give access to the court. Their cedar crownings are composed of thousands of those little compartments, geometrically juxtaposed, which have the appearance of the wax honeycombs patiently constructed by the bees; but over the general arrangement of these innumerable little things, an indefinable something has presided, which is the genius of Arab art, and has fashioned them into a harmoniously simple whole. All the crownings of the doorways are crowded, like very large balconies, crowded almost to

breaking point, by white-veiled women, who
lean over, silently, to watch us.

The court, naturally, is paved with mosaics
and marble, and in the centre a fountain plays.
It is filled, vibrant, with an exalted music, at
once rapid and grave : very high human voices,
accompanied by powerful stringed instruments,
tabours and iron castanets. We recognise the
same orchestra as the other day was at the
house of the Vizier of War; it is in fact one of
the Sultan's, and he has lent it in our honour.

. . . .

He is extraordinarily handsome, the Kaid El-
Meshwar, our host. The description of Matho,
in " Salammbô ": " A colossal Lybian," etc.,
would fit him perfectly. He is of superhuman
stature and size, and his features and eyes are
admirable. His beard is already grey, and his
dark skin bears witness, despite the regularity
of his features, to a strain of black blood.
Beauty, in fact, is the principal qualification
required in a Kaid El-Meshwar; the post is
almost always given to the most superb speci-
men of a man in Morocco.

Like his colleague of war, this vizier does
not sit at table with us, for a good Mussulman
is not supposed to eat with Nazarenes. He is
content to sit in the shadow, near the hall in
which our luncheon is served, and see to it that

his slaves, bewildered by our presence, provide us with mountains of couscous and other eatables.

During the monster repast, I face the beautiful court, which is disclosed to me in its entirety by the high denticulated arch of the doorway. The Soudanese slaves, in large earrings and bracelets, cross it in an endless stream, bearing on their heads the gigantic dishes, surmounted by roofings like the gables of turrets. The mosaics of the pavement sparkle with light. Here and there, in the high walls, through pierced loopholes, I see confusedly the eyes of women shining. The wall at the back, which rises like a screen against the sun, is crowned with veiled heads watching us. And the music, in an extreme exaltation, repeats, repeats unceasingly, in a growing precipitancy, the same monotonous phrases which, in time, soothe, magnetise, induce a kind of stupor.

.   .   .   .

Two o'clock in the afternoon, the sun at its hottest.

As I leave to-morrow, I venture forth even at this burning hour, for I have a thousand and one things to do on this last day.

I have first to go to the walled town of the Jews, where horribly sordid old men, cunning and sinister in their ugliness, hold, in the depth of their dens, ancient jewels, rare arms, and

stuffs not to be found even in the bazaar, which
I desire to buy from them.

It is a considerable distance away, this Jewish
town ; it runs, in a narrow strip, along the
southern side of New Fez, and I live in Old
Fez, from which I must needs first of all emerge.

I am on horseback, escorted by a red guard.

Two o'clock in the afternoon, on one of the
hottest days we have yet had. The old earthen
walls seem to be dried up by the devouring sun,
the old crevices in the houses seem to grow
larger and more open. The little streets are
deserted between their two rows of dead ruins
which are cracking in the heat; the paving-
stones, the old black cobbles, polished by the
bare feet and slippers of many Arab generations,
show in places their shining heads amid waste
straw and dust. And over all the somnolent
town is that silent prostration which is peculiar
to the moments when the sun dazzles and burns.

There is a little shade and coolness as we
pass under the thick triple gates of the ramparts. In the recesses of these gates, barbers
are installed on the ground, in process of shaving
some woolly-headed, wild-looking countrymen,
one of whom holds by the horns, while he is
being shaved, two black rams. And in another corner a practitioner is " bleeding " a
shepherd (like cupping formerly with us, it is

a cure for all ills ; the incision is made with a
razor at the back of the neck and goes to the
bone of the skull). To-day, more even than
usual, I am struck by the wildness of these
approaches to Fez, by their silence, their air
of mournful abandonment.

And, once through the gates, there begins
immediately a burning desert without roads,
to-day without a human being, without a
caravan. This is the place that was so crowded
and so brilliant on the morning of our pompous
arrival ; now one hears no more than the little,
mournful voices of the grasshoppers. Town
walls and palace walls rise everywhere into
the sky, in an imposing confusion, with their
battlements, their bristling points of stone.
All straight, all alike, mournful and sombre
from base to summit, contriving to produce an
impression of beauty by virtue of their gigantic
size. And at their foot, nothing ; on this side
of the town, nothing within sight, not a house,
not a tree, not a tent, not a group of men ; the
walls alone, upright and immense in vertical
stature. The implacable sun of to-day accentuates their extreme antiquity, their cracks,
their crevices ; in places they are dismantled,
breached, and their base is corroded.

And other walls completely ruinous, infinitely desolate, part from these ramparts,

ramify, prolong the town into the deserted campaign, and end by becoming confused with the rocks, the ruins, the quagmires, with all the litter of this old soil dug and dug again in the course of centuries. Time has covered these walls with a bright yellow lichen, which shows on the dun grey of the stones like a scattering of golden stains; under the deep blue of the sky the whole is of a warm and ardent tone, with trimmings of brocade.

In the part utterly downfallen, in the secondary walls which in their decrepitude have outlived their purpose, there are gateways exquisite in form, like all Arab gateways, and surrounded with mosaics visible still between the coatings of lichen; they give access to kinds of deserted prison-yards, where one finds only weeds and grasshoppers.

As I go on horseback round these debris of ramparts in the magnificent, overpowering sunshine, I am brought to a standstill before one of these gateways, which impresses me as the most exquisitely Arab thing that I have ever seen: in the middle of some hundred yards of monotonous and formidable wall, it opens its isolated ogive, framed with mysterious designs; and at its side a date-palm, old and solitary, lifts on high its bouquet of yellowed plumes.

.   .   .   .

A hundred yards farther on the Sultan's camp appears. Beyond in the campaign its tents make masses or sowings of white things in the midst of reddish-brown plains and blue distances—and all these whitenesses are a-tremble in the hot air. The camp is considerably augmented since last I saw it. When complete it has a circumference, I am told, of nearly four miles, and contains thirty thousand men.

The Caliph's tent is in the middle, lofty and immense. One sees only the canvas wall, called the *tarabieh*, which serves it as enclosure, concealing everything within. (Even in war, the dwelling of the Caliph must be a hidden thing.) Behind this wall, it seems, is quite a little town; besides the particular abode of the sovereign and its dependencies, there is that of his favourite child, the little Abd-ul-Aziz; and also those of a certain number of ladies of the harem chosen to take part in the journey.

As soon as the Sultan's tent issues from the lumber-rooms of the palace, and begins to be erected outside the walls, the news is spread throughout the whole of Morocco by passing caravans and, more especially, by those swift "runners" who travel night and day, across mountains and across rivers, carrying letters and news, and performing the function of our post. All the tribes are informed betimes that

the sovereign is about to set out for war, and
the rebels prepare themselves for resistance.

The Sultan, we know, spends generally six
months of the year under his tent, a nomad
by nature like his Arabian ancestors, waging a
ceaseless war in his own empire against re-
volted tribes who recognise him as a religious
caliph, but not always as a sovereign ; some
of them indeed (the Zemur, for example, and
the Riff tribes) have never been subjugated.

On this occasion the Sultan will not return
to Fez for four years. In the intervals of his
forays and harvests of heads he will rest in
his two other capitals, Mekinez and Morocco,
where, as here, he possesses palaces and
impenetrable gardens.

Accordingly, during the past week, those of his
women who are not to take part in his pending
travels were sent in advance, on muleback
and in three detachments, to the walled
seraglios of Mekinez.

.   .   .   .

I shall have time and to spare to visit the
sordid Jewish town, which was indeed the ob-
jective of my ride, and the desire comes to me
to ascend a last point in the mountain that
overlooks Old Fez.

By little rocky pathways my horse climbs
hardily, even making high-spirited attempts at

galloping. And very soon we are at the top, inhaling a keen, fresh breeze, which passes over carpetings of flowers and sets them moving. From distance to distance there are trees in the windings of the ground; in kinds of little valleys there are spreading tufts of olives, in the shadow of which blackamoor shepherds are singing pastoral songs to their goats in the mournful silence of the landscape. Above all there are tombs, tombs everywhere, old, old tombs, amongst rank weeds and aloes. There are *koubas* of saints, venerated ruins, the graceful porticoes of which are haunted by hosts of birds. And there is the historic kiosk that was built by a sultan of old and cost him his throne. For the people of Fez, always easily incensed, took it ill that he should see, from above, their women of evenings on the terraces.

All these terraces, in fact, are disclosed to me from here, thousands of grey promenades, empty at this hour of the sun's dazzlement. I command the view of the holy town, its long lines of crumbling walls, its bastions and battlements, its minarets and isolated palms. Two or three rows of donkeys and camels, departing in file for I know not what southern country, alone animate its solitary approaches. And all this is bathed, flooded, with an immense light; in the sky, lost here and there in the infinite blue, are a few little fleecy clouds, and that is all.

And no noise ascends from the town, over which broods still the same immobility, the same torpor.

.   .   .   .

I turn my steps at last towards the Jewish town in quest of old tapestries and old arms. For here, as in our Europe of the Middle Ages, it is the Jews who hold in their coffers not only the gold, the fortunes, but the precious stones, the antique jewels, and also all sorts of other old, valuable things that the embarrassed viziers and kaids have ended by leaving on their hands. And, with it all, affecting airs of poverty; disdained by the Arabs even more than by the Christians, living on the sly, cooped within their darksome, narrow quarter, fearful, and for ever on guard for their life.

Descended from the luminous mountain where so many saints and dervishes lie sleeping under the flowers, I follow for some time the walls, astonishingly old, of New Fez—by pathways at first bare and barren, but soon verdant and shady, with mulberry-trees and poplars that have donned once more their tiny, fresh green leaves of April; with clear streams running amongst drenched reeds, irises and large white bindweed.

Q

The ramparts of the Jews are as high and as embattled as those of the Arabs, their arched gateways are as large, with the same heavy gates overlaid with iron. These gates are shut early every evening; Israelite guards, mistrustful of air, stand in the embrasures, allowing no suspicious-looking person to pass. One realises that life in this cave is spent in perpetual fear of neighbours, Arabs and Berbers.

And before the entrance to their town is the general dumping-ground of dead beasts (a compliment that is paid to them). To enter it is necessary to pass between heaps of dead horses, dead dogs, carcasses of all descriptions, rotting in the sun, and shedding an odour without a name. They are not allowed to remove them —and at night there is a grand concert of jackals under the walls. Nor from the narrow streets, so narrow that one can scarcely pass, are they allowed to remove the refuse thrown from the houses; for months bones, pickings of vegetables, all sorts of rubbish, are heaped up, until it pleases an Arab councillor, moved to it by a large sum of money, to have them cleared away. In this dark, damp quarter the odours are of a class apart, and the faces of the inhabitants all are pale.

Two or three persons standing at this entrance of the town watch my arrival, curious to learn

what may be the object of my visit. They stare
at me shrewdly, with crafty, covetous eyes, as
if they scented business afoot; wretched-looking
faces, long and narrow and pallid; thin, interminable noses and long sparse hair hanging in
straggling ringlets on to greasy, bedandruffed
black robes that cling closely to angular
shoulders.

So much the worse for the precious stuffs and
the old arms. I cannot bring myself to plunge
into these mouldy dens, amongst creatures so
ugly, on the eve of my departure, on so fair a
last day, when the sun gilds so radiantly the
tranquillities of the Mussulman town and its
old imposing walls.

I turn aside, therefore, at this gateway of the
Jewish quarter, and make my way towards the
Sultan's palace. I shall reach it at the time
when all the great personages, clothed in white,
are leaving after the evening audience, to return
to their homes in Fez-Bali; and shall see once
more that procession of figures of another age,
in the magnificent setting of great walled courtyards and monumental ruins.

.   .   .   .

Here, again, are the approaches to the
palace; the walls and the walls, all straight,
all grim, and all alike. Here are the series of
mournful courtyards, empty and vast as parade

grounds, and yet seeming almost narrow, so high are the walls that enclose them. To realise their dimensions it is necessary to observe the men, the few white phantoms that cross them and seem astonishingly small.

The sun is setting as we reach, my guard and I, the first of these enclosures, which is already filled with shadow. The high walls, the high gloomy walls, masking everything, suddenly lower the light like immense screens. With their alignment of sharp points they look menacing and cruel. Beyond, in the middle of the opposite wall, the large archway leading farther into these fastnesses opens, flanked by its four square towers, which seem all of a piece, awe-inspiring after the manner of the donjon of Vincennes, but with an air of added wickedness by reason of their crowning of points of stone.

The ground of this courtyard is sprinkled with stones, with all sorts of debris, with holes and bones. Two or three camels move about it in quest of the sparse grass, looking quite little at the foot of things so high and grand. Lost in a corner there is an encampment of white tents like a pigmy village. And three grave personages, draped in burnouses, issuing beyond, from the darkness of the great gateway, seem to me Lilliputian. In the air there

are the inevitable storks, which cross the empty
square outlined on the sky by the dark teeth of
the battlements. And thousands, thousands
of birds, of a glistening black, cling in clusters
on the walls, all touching one another, pushing
one another, clambering one upon the other,
forming swarming patches, like the massings
of flies that in summer descend upon things
unclean. And while I stand watching these
gatherings of little wings and little claws, the
three grave personages, advancing across the
courtyard, approach me : three greybeards who
smile good-humouredly and vouchsafe me, in
Arabic, information about these birds, which
I do not understand. (This affability of casual
passers-by to an unknown Nazarene is not an
everyday occurrence in a country like Morocco ;
that is my excuse for mentioning so insignificant
an adventure.)

I direct my steps towards the gateway
opposite. It will bring me to a second enclosure, usually more animated, where each
day the white-robed viziers administer justice
to the people. O these Arab gateways, so
infinitely various in their mysterious designs !
How can I tell the charm there is for me in
their mere aspect, the kind of religious melancholy, the reverie of bygone times that one and
all awaken in me ; isolated in the middle of

walls as heart-breaking as the walls of prisons;
having in their ogival form, whether festooned
or round, I know not what indefinable quality
which remains always the same, in the midst
of the most fantastic diversity; and always
framed with those delicate geometrical orna-
mentations, the rare gracefulness of which
has in it something severe and ideally pure,
something in the highest degree mystical.

The new enclosure into which this gate leads
me is as large, as imposing, as forbidding as
the first. But it is, as I expected, full of people,
and the approaches to it are encumbered with
peaked-saddled horses and mules, held by
servants. It is on the farther side of the courtyard, under old archways forming alcoves of
stone, that the ministers officiate, scarcely
sheltered from the wind, and with a minimum
of scribes, a minimum of documents.

Under one of these archways is the Vizier of
War. Under the other the Vizier of Justice
delivers out of hand judgments against which
there can be no appeal. Around him, some
soldiers, by a lusty use of sticks, keep back
the crowd, and the accused, the prisoners,
the plaintiffs, the witnesses, without any
discrimination, are brought before him in the
same manner, clutched at the scruff of the
neck by two athletic guards.

As these quarters are considered unsafe
for Nazarenes, I remain at the entrance, lest
I should become the cause of diplomatic
complications.

But at this hour, as I anticipated, the session
is at an end. One after another, the viziers,
assisted by their servants, mount their mules
to return to their homes. White beards, long
white robes, long white veils; white mules,
with red cloth saddles, each led by four slaves
clothed all in white, with high, red caps. And,
while the crowd disperses, they depart, slowly,
calmly, with the lofty dignity of old prophets,
their gaze rapt in sombre meditation, snowy
in their whitenesses, against the background of
the great ramparts, the great ruins. The sun
is sinking, and, as every evening, under the
sky turned suddenly yellow, a cold wind rises,
blusters through the high archways, whistles
over the old stones.

Behind the viziers I too retire. For one
last time I want to see the marvels of my
terrace at the holy hour of Moghreb.

.   .   .   .

Above, on my housetop, there is the same
enchantment as every evening: the town a
blend of pale and ruddy gold, the neighbouring
terraces separated from mine by an intangible
blue vapour, and the distant terraces, the

thousands of rainbow-tinted squares of stone that dwindle, sloping on the hillsides like things overthrown, down to the girdle of the ramparts and green gardens. All the negress slaves are there, at their posts, their faces black and smiling, coiffed in spotless white or rose-coloured scarves. And there, too, are all my fair neighbours of the tall *hantouze*, leaning on their elbows, or reclining, or proudly upright, very graceful of face and very brilliant of colour, with their broad stiff waistbands, their long hanging sleeves, and all that floats behind them, golden scarves and unbound hair. And once more, just as it has done for centuries and centuries, the great prayer rings out in mournfully prolonged voices, while the snows of the Atlas fade on the pale yellow of the sky.

.   .   .   .

At night, after dinner, by lantern-light, I leave my house exceptionally to go, before the hour at which the gates of the quarters are closed, to bid adieu to the Minister and the embassy. They have to remain here for I know not how much longer.

Captain H. de V*** and I are to set out to-morrow in the morning twilight. Each of us has been presented, on behalf of the Sultan, with a tent, a picked mule and an Arab saddle; and in addition a tent for our servants, a kaid to guide us, and eight mules and muleteers to carry our treasures and baggage.

In lantern-light, also, I find the embassy installed as usual in the grove of fragrant orange-trees, under the verandah of the beautiful old kiosk. His Excellency has duly received for us the letter, signed by the Sultan and sealed with his seal, which is our passport through the territories of the different tribes, and gives us the indispensable right of *mouna*. But in spite of the efforts he has been good enough to make, he has not yet obtained the letter to the chiefs of the town of Mekinez, nor the permit to visit there the " gardens of Aguedal." It is not nnwillingness, I know quite well ; it is dilatoriness, inertia. The Grand Vizier was too late, it seems, to get the Sultan's signature before the hour of prayer. He has promised that by to-morrow morning everything shall be signed and in order, and that, if we have already started, horsemen shall follow in our wake, to Mekinez, if needs be, bearing the desiderated documents, with certain presents that are intended for us. But we scarcely believe it and are disappointed.

Our travelling companions, who are remaining at Fez, are a little grieved that they are not coming with us. Their sojourn here is like to be much longer than they expected. There are a thousand and one complicated matters to be put straight; disputes going back for a number of years, Jewish loans that can never be repaid. With this people, things come not to an issue. The Sultan is almost always invisible, entrenched like an idol in his impenetrable palace. And the viziers temporise, to gain time being the great art of Mussulman diplomacy. And now the month of Ramadan is drawing near, during which nothing can be done; already one begins to feel its influence. It is only very early in the morning that affairs can be discussed, and then only piecemeal, and with all the customary Oriental circumlocution. The middle of the day is given up to prayer and sleep—and the evening to domestic concerns. Then, too, one of the most important of the political personages has lately been bitten in the arm by one of his numerous white wives, jealous of one of his numerous black ones. He is confined to his bed, and there is a delay the more.

We that are about to depart are charged with commissions for Tangier; for the modern, living world from which here one seems so far away. Those that remain are smitten already, it is easy to see, with that curious malady, that yearning to depart, which is in no way new. It seems infallibly to attack the members of an embassy at the end of a fortnight passed in Fez. It is, moreover, a political circumstance on which the Arab diplomats have learnt to count. Even I, who would so willingly remain, can sympathise with this feeling, for there have been moments when I have experienced myself the oppression of Islam.

CHAPTER XXXII

28th April.

THE dawn is a very grey one for the morning of our departure.

Awakened in the early twilight in my old, old house, I examine with some uneasiness the square of gloomy sky that appears through the gaping opening in my roof. It is charged with threatening rain.

Around me there are now no rugs, no hangings, no token of my fleeting occupation; everything has been removed and packed up; the air of antiquity and mournful dilapidation has returned once more.

I have arranged with Captain H. de V*** that we shall travel in burnouses, so as less to attract the attention of the tribes in passing. And as my native wardrobe was not in very good condition, I have had my long flowing robes, my long white *faradjias* washed in preparation for the journey, and they have passed the night hung out on my terrace to dry.

I go up to get them in the pale light of the growing day, smiling a little to think how this homely detail identifies me for a moment with the existence of a real Arab of the poorer class preparing for the road.

They are still damp, my *faradjias*, and strike very cold when I put them on.

From the height of my roof I can observe that the sky is uniformly cloudy, a broad expanse of unbroken grey. A profound silence, very mournful, very solemn, weighs yet at this matutinal hour on the scarcely enlightened town. I bid good-bye for ever to all the surrounding terraces, which are empty now and dismal; good-bye to all the old ruinous walls of round-about, behind which my fair neighbours are still sleeping, including the sweet rebel of whom I shall know no more.

At five o'clock my saddled mule arrives before my door, led by one of the Sultan's soldiers. It is pitch dark in the deep-lying street. I am to meet H. de V*** and our muleteers and baggage outside the gate of the town, which is at some distance from my house. For the last time, therefore, I make my way through the dark little streets of Fez, in the midst of a compact multitude of oxen (the herds that are brought in at night for fear of robbers and wild beasts, and taken out again to their pastures in the early hours of the morning).

. . . .

Leaving the enclosure of Old Fez by the high black ogives, I follow now the antiquated ramparts of New Fez. The mournfulness of the high walls, the mournfulness of the quagmires, the mournfulness of the ruins, all this is augmented this morning by the grey half-light and the silence. I hear about me only the trotting of the herds of oxen by which I am surrounded ; the breath issues from their nostrils in whitish puffs. The herdsmen who drive them, their hoods drawn down, are draped, like dead men, in grey, earth-stained rags.

Here are the gloomy portals of the palace. Out of them, one after another, come some hundred black slaves, carrying on their heads those esparto turrets, which always conceal gigantic dishes, and, in their wake, an odour of couscous piping hot spreads in the fresh morning air. For to-day is a great Mussulman feast-day preceding the fasts of Ramadan, something like our Shrove Tuesday, and it is the custom on this day for the Sultan to send to all the dignitaries of the town a dish prepared in his own kitchens.

Captain H. de V*** is at the meeting-place outside the gate of Old Fez, with our mules, our tents, our little escort. And nearly all our companions of the embassy are there too, early on horseback, to accompany us on the first stage of our journey.

Outside the walls we salute in passing the Sultan's camp and his high, closed tent. Then we set out, under the grey sky, along those kinds of irregular tracks that have been beaten in course of time by the tramp of the caravans. Sad, sombre colours everywhere, accentuating the desolate grandeur of the approaches to the town. A mist hangs low over the immense plain of barley, infinitely green ; a plain which seems to be bounded on all sides by a confused obscurity, an opaque blackness which mounts into the sky and is made of high mountains buried in clouds.

On this same sombre background Fez gradually diminishes, takes on that same sinister aspect which has remained in our memory since its first appearance on the morning of our arrival. Turning in the saddle, we can see for some time yet, at the foot of its blackish walls, the rows of little snow-white cones which are the camp of the thrice holy Caliph.

Sad, sombre colours everywhere ; the wayfarers enveloped in wool, the camels, the donkeys, all that comes and goes between the two towns by this one and only road is earthy, brown or grey in colour. From time to time we pass little Bedouin encampments—the tents

of the same brown colour as the ground—from
which little columns of smoke rise straight
against the dark grey of the distances. And,
above, high up, the blithe skylark, invisible in
the mist, sings his morning song, sings it lustily,
over green fields of barley, as in France.

.　　.　　.　　.　　.　　.　　.

At the first *m'safa*, our French friends leave
us with good wishes for our journey, and return
to Fez. And we proceed, alone for many days,
with our little escort of Arabs.

Between Fez and Mekinez there are thirteen
m'safa—that is to say, thirteen stages—marked
each by a well of drinkable water, which opens
without the least warning, in the middle of the
track. The journey is generally made in two
days, or sometimes three, when the ladies of
the seraglio travel. We are counting on arriving this evening, even early this evening, with
our picked and quite fresh mules.

Soon the cultivated fields come to an end.
Then begins a plain of fennel, immense, un-
limited ; the giant fennel of Africa, the flowering
stems of which are eight or nine feet high, are
as tall as trees. We seem to be entering a
yellow forest, prolonged on all sides, up to those
obstinately black, opaque, imprisoning distances, which are always the same mountains
smothered in the same clouds.

And all along these little ill-marked pathways we brush against this fennel; it overtops us, caressing us with its fresh leaves, as fine and wavy as the feathers of a marabou; we are buried in its frail green and yellow network, we disappear beneath it, inhaling its odour to excess.

In the air the merry larks continue to sing distractedly, soaring high, invisible in the grey mist. And from distance to distance, at intervals of two or three miles perhaps, a tall isolated palm-tree rises above this uniform and deserted grove.

For some four hours we proceed thus through the forest of fennel. Sometimes, ahead of us, on the track everywhere buried under the thicknesses of fine green down, we hear a rustling that is not ours, and presently there emerges, from amongst the masses of outspread leaves, a herd of cattle which passes us, or a file of burnoused gentlemen coming from Mekinez, or a caravan. It is always a droll business to meet camels, especially in a narrow place. You think you are still some distance from them, from the long legs and the central mass of the body, when the head is already upon you, at the end of the outstretched, undulating neck; and this head stares at you from quite near, with an expression of bored contempt. They stop

R

for a moment the better to see you, then turn away and continue their wonted slow and silent motion. They have an indefinable odour, sweet and musty, midway between a stench and a perfume; and they leave a trail of it behind them, even long after they have passed.

We are making this return journey on mule-back—which seems less dignified than to be on horseback, as we came, but is the only really practical and really Arab manner of travelling in Morocco. It allows us, moreover, to keep in sight throughout our tents and baggage, which follow at the same pace, at the same gait, on beasts of the same kind. We have not now as at the setting out a pompous escort, some three or four hundred horsemen with guards marshalled along the route. We travel in a closed-up file, a little cortège of a dozen men, and as many beasts, and have ourselves to keep an eye on everything, a little lost as we are in the midst of these deserted expanses.

Our saddles, covered in red cloth, are very large and very hard, and while our mules continue their swift, incessant, indefatigable course, we quickly learn to assume upon them, like the Moroccans, all the known positions of travel: astraddle, seated, asprawl, or with legs crossed along the beast's neck. From time to time the muleteers recount to us stories of brigands, pointing out the spots where travellers have been robbed or murdered. For the rest of the day they sing strange little songs, in a shrill piping falsetto, reminiscent of grass-hoppers or birds; and their monotonous little music harmonises mournfully with the profound silence of the solitudes.

At the end of these four hours, passed in the fennel, we reach the edge of a gigantic fissure which serpentines in the plain: a ravine, an abyss, at the bottom of which a torrent rolls. We follow its course, against the current of the waters, until we reach a waterfall, above which the torrent is no more than a rapidly flowing river. It is the Oued Mahouda. Just above the clamorous cascade, which in a single leap falls some hundred feet into the void, we cross the river by a deep and dangerous ford, lifting our legs on to the necks of our mules, which are up to their middle in the agitated and noisy water.

.   .   .   .

This ford marks the half-way between the two holy cities, and is very much frequented by Moroccan travellers.

We halt for some time on the farther bank, one of our Arabs continuing meanwhile his journey to Mekinez in order to advise the pasha of our approach, as is fitting for the travellers of quality that we are.

Our halting-place is just above the boisterous waterfall, overlooking on one side the ford by which the caravans cross, and on the other the ravine into which the headlong waters fall, and falling seethe. The country around is decked in the green of springtime, and the sides of the ravine are pink with hanging garlands of bindweed. The grey clouds have lifted, still veiling the sky, but leaving the terrestrial distances unobscured and clear.

In addition to the wayfarers, on horseback or afoot, who every now and then cross by the ford, there comes a whole nomad tribe—men, beasts and tents. The women of this *douar*, who are the last to pass, tuck their clothes up to the waist with a naïve disregard of modesty, revealing their shapely, statuesque legs, a little yellow and in places a little tattooed. But they keep their faces chastely veiled.

We get under way again. A region of mountains and rocks comes first. Then another ford, in a setting of a strangeness all its own : it is in the face of an infinitely deserted plain, and at the foot of a mass of rocks on which some old men, motionless as Termini, sit in isolation. They give no heed to us, and seem to be solitary mystics absorbed in contemplation.

.   .   .   .

Follow four hours of regions absolutely wild,

deserts of dwarf palms and daffodils like those
we traversed so endlessly on our way out.
Often we turn in the saddle to count our little
troop, to see that none of our muleteers, none
of our pack-mules, is missing from the muster,
for we are still very uncertain of the fidelity
of our men. And on this level plain, covered
as it is with a short vegetation, our close-going
caravan is easy to embrace in a single glance,
seems even quite little, quite isolated, quite lost.

At the head of the little column rides gravely
the kaid answerable for our heads : an old man,
in a caftan of pink cloth under a transparent
garment of white muslin. His eyes are lustre-
less, are dead ; his face, hard, accentuated,
looks as if it had been rough-hewn out of brown
wood, and his white beard is like a lichen on a
ruin. He is upright, expressionless, majestically
mummified on his white mule, carrying cross-
wise on his saddle his long brass gun.

Mekinez ! On the limit of the desolate plain,
seeming still very far away, Mekinez appears.
One realises that one sees it only by virtue of
the unbroken lines of the ground and the wonderful clearness of the air. It is a little blackish
band — the walls, no doubt — above which
bristle, scarcely visible, slender as reeds, the
towers of the mosques.

·   ·   ·   ·   ·   ·   ·

We ride on for some time yet, until we reach a point where the view is hidden from us by old, crumbling walls, which seem to enclose immense parks. We are at the outskirts of the town. Through a breach we enter these enclosures, to find ourselves in a region of olive-trees planted regularly in quincunxes, and on soil covered with very fine grass and moss, such as is only met with in places that have long been tranquil, untrodden by men. These olives, moreover, are exhausted, dying, covered with a kind of mouldiness, a malady of age, which turns their foliage black, as if it had been smoked. And the enclosures follow one another, always in ruins, confining these same phantoms of trees aligned in all directions as far as eye can see. They might be a series of parks abandoned for centuries, promenades for the dead.

And thus it comes upon us as an odd surprise to see, as we pass, in one of these mournful little alleys a group of little burnouses of brilliant colours, green, orange, blue and red, which tell of children in their bravest toggery. Behind them, a number of white-veiled women encircle a coil of grey smoke, which ascends from the ground towards the branches. Our Arabs explain to us that it is a day of annual treat and picnic for the schoolchildren of Mekinez; they

are here for a day in the country, decked all in
their finest clothes. The white veils seen in the
background of the picture represent the mothers
who accompany them ; the smoke is that of the
rustic supper that has been prepared for them
on the smooth sward ; and now their picnic is
over ; they are about to depart, in order to
return to the town before nightfall.

I think it is one of the most unexpected, most
charming, and at the same time most pathetic
things that I have met with in the course of
my journey, this children's festival, the brilliance
of these little gaily coloured burnouses in movement on the tender, smooth turf of this desolate
park.

. . . .

As we issue from these walls and these olives,
Mekinez suddenly reappears, very close to us now
and immense, crowning with its grey shadow
a succession of hills behind which the sun is
setting. We are separated from the town only
by a ravine of verdure, a medley of poplars,
mulberry-trees, orange-trees, any trees you will,
all in their fresh tints of April.

Very high against the yellow sky show
the lines of the superposed ramparts, the
innumerable terraces, the minarets, the towers
of the mosques, the formidable embattled
kasbahs, and, above a number of fortress walls,

the green-tiled roof of the Sultan's palace. It is even more imposing than Fez, and more solemn. But it is only a phantom of a town, a mass of ruins and rubbish, inhabited by scarce more than five or six thousand souls, Arabs, Berbers and Jews.

During the long halt of midday, our men told us we should arrive for the hour of Moghreb. And, in fact, just as we appear, the white flag is hoisted on all the minarets. The "*Allah Ak'bar!*" resounds in awesome clamour over the whole extent of the town, even into the dead countryside around. And, in the hearing of these long, mournful cries, this Allah, whom these men implore, seems to us for the moment so grand and so terrible that we too feel an impulse to prostrate ourselves on the ground, at the summons of the muezzin, before his gloomy eternity.

.   .   .   .

The horseman whom we had sent as estafette returns to meet us, having seen the pasha, having received his instructions regarding the place of our encampment. It is outside the walls, needless to say.

Led by this guide, we cross the green ravine, the delightful medley of trees that separates us from the town. Then for a long time, interminably it seems, we skirt, without entering, the old crenellated ramparts. They have a height of fifty or sixty feet, and are corroded at the base, cracked and decrepit. In the kind of circumjacent track we follow, no one passes ; the most we encounter are three or four beggars huddled like corpses in the angles of the bastions ; hideous and appalling in their tattered burnouses ; miserable wretches covered with excoriated sores, with I know not what leprosy. On the ground are a number of dead, half-devoured beasts, mules, horses, camels, the open belly wide agape, and bones everywhere, strewn about by the jackals, and heaps of refuse and rotting offal.

At length, some five hundred yards from a gateway, on a bare, deserted ground sprinkled with ruins and holes and scattered stones, we are brought to a halt : we have arrived at the spot assigned to us for a resting-place.

It is at the foot of one of those gigantic walls which, here as at Fez, stretch far into the campaign, without affording any indication of what may once have been their object. And here, very quickly, our little canvas houses are set up, in the yellow twilight, what time a few drops of rain begin to fall from heavy clouds, which suddenly have overspread the sky.

The crushing wall against which we have pitched our camp is pierced with a row of high porticoes, some half stopped with masonry, others wide open on to the dark, treacherous countryside. And this wall, following an upward slope, leads, beyond, to the ramparts of Mekinez, to the nearest gate, which is, it seems, one of the principal entrances to the town. No road leads to this gate, it needs not to say; no one enters it, and no one leaves; nothing seems to live, and, since the great prayer of a few moments ago, we hear no movement, no noise, no more than if there were nothing around but abandoned ruins.

It is unspeakable, the melancholy of this end of rampart wall that one sees from here, crowning a hill, and crowned in turn by an old minaret—the melancholy of this city gate which, like a black figuring, frames in its pointed arch a little yellow patch of still luminous sky.

This end of rampart wall, this minaret, and this arch, are all that we see to-night of Mekinez, the holy city.

. . . .

Near our camp there are two stone fountains, extremely old, with troughs out of which the camels drink. Before the night finally descends we go, in the light of a lantern, to obtain there a supply of fresh water. They are ornamented, these fountains, with exquisite festooned arabesques, which are crumbling to dust.

Arrives now, mounted on a superb horse, and preceded by a large perforated lantern, the son of the pasha of the town. He is come to bid us welcome, and to present the excuses of his father, who is absent. For two months now, this old, holy person, at the head of his cavaliers, has been warring against the terrible Zemur, who are desolating the country.

The son is very young, very pleasant; he announces a plentiful *mouna*, with hot cous-cous, that he is sending us—and also some soldiers to guard us till morning. As a pre-liminary, two little donkeys follow close upon him, laden, one with charcoal, the other with branches, to enable us to cook the chickens in the open.

He stays sitting in our tent, regaling us with stories. Concerning this wall, at the foot of which we are, he has no clear notion of what may once have been its purpose. He knows only that it was built by Mulai-Ismail, the Cruel Sultan, three hundred years ago. The great days of Mekinez, indeed, date back to this Mulai-Ismail, who was the most glorious of the sultans of Morocco.

After the young pasha a Jew also comes to visit us, in the now pitch dark night, preceded by an escort and a large lantern. Despite his simple brown robe, he is, we are told, the richest man in the town. His face, too, is distinguished-looking, regular and extremely kind. He had been advised of our coming, some days before, by a messenger from one of his co-religionists in Tangier, a Monsieur Benchimol, who, during the whole journey of the mission, has shown to each one of us an inexhaustible kindness—and he comes very courteously to place himself at our disposal. We promise to call upon him to-morrow, and, in haste, he withdraws, for fear of finding the old gates of the ramparts shut against him.

Around our tents the ground is uneven, ex-foliated, as in the approaches to towns of great antiquity; there are entrances to underground passages, crevasses; above all there are little grassy mounds, sufficiently singular of aspect, providing food for thought. It needs the utmost precaution to take even two steps outside the tent in the darkness. The jackals, the owls, all the mournful-voiced inhabitants of the caves and the old walls of roundabout give us one after another a warning of their presence, by some isolated cry that sounds like a little call of death. And the rain now falls steadily, as if the surroundings of our camp were not dismal enough already.

Half-past eight. — *Nine o'clock.* — Our two

visitors retired long ago, but nothing comes of what should have been sent to us, neither *mouna* nor guards. Mekinez, no doubt, has closed its gates for fear of robbers, and has forgotten us outside, at the mercy of all sorts of men and adventures. Truly we find it very black and very silent around our little canvas houses, under this overcast sky which makes the night doubly dark, and in proximity to the walls of this strange dead city.

At last, at long last, some lanterns shine in the distance, having issued no doubt from the gateway cut out above, in the ramparts. They descend towards us, by the kind of irregular, rugged avenue where caverns yawn. It is our *mouna* coming to us, slow and grave as ever: a milk couscous, a sugar couscous; a live sheep and a number of chickens in cages. Willingly would we send back the poor beasts, were such a course permissible to us; but they must needs be delivered up to the knife and the voracity of the men of our escort.

Other lanterns now appear on the height and descend towards us: an armed troop, beating a drum. They are the soldiers coming to guard us until sunrise; and from their number—at least eighty—one may judge either that the young pasha is very prudent, or else that the place has a very evil reputation.

They sit down in a circle around our tents, on the dubious grass or on the indeterminate dark things, and begin to sing to keep themselves in watchfulness, facing one another two by two. They will sing till morning; it is the custom with all the nocturnal guards who do their duty conscientiously, and we must manage to get to sleep as best we can in the midst of this savage choir which will never make an end.

.   .   .   .

Towards midnight their music becomes a discordant cacophony of an altogether disrespectful kind. To mount guard over " Nazarenes " has been too much for their gravity; they no longer sing, they imitate all the beasts of Morocco—the cries of dogs, of camels, of laying hens—and diversify them with bellowings of pure fantasy. Then I get up, furious. Gropingly, I go and awaken in his tent the old kaid in charge, and, together, he with a lantern, I a riding-whip, we make the round of the guards, using threats of immediate punishment, of complaint to the pasha, of cudgellings, of prison even. And, docilely, silence supervenes.

.   .   .   .

One o'clock in the morning.—A second *mouna* is brought to us, more pompous than the first : an immense couscous of dessert, pyramids of cakes, hampers of oranges, tea and loaves of sugar. The young pasha has set himself to do things well. The men of our escort get up and begin again an all-devouring feast, and we end by falling asleep.

CHAPTER XXXIII

29th April.

AWAKENING under a gloomy sky, we perceive
that we are encamped in a cemetery : a cemetery
of the poor, probably, for around us are no
tombstones, but merely little mounds sparsely
covered with grass, some very old, others still
new. And we have slept above these dead.

There is no more movement than yesterday
in the approaches to the town. On the height
beyond, in the great ogive of the entrance which
opens in the middle of the ramparts, nothing
living is to be seen, and the mournful desert
begins at once, from the foot of the long walls.

At about eight o'clock, however, three or
four Jews appear, recognisable in the distance
from their black robes. Leaving the gateway,
they make their way down to our camp over
the greyish, exfoliated and stone-strewn ground.
They have come to offer us trinkets and old-
world embroideries, which they unpack on the
ground, on the damp grass, amongst the pegs
and ropes of our tents.

. . . .

Nine o'clock.—A horseman, covered with

272

dust, who seems to have ridden hard, arrives from Fez. He brings us what we have been waiting for in order to enter the holy city : the letters from the Sultan to the pasha and the amins according us the privilege of passing through Mekinez and of visiting the mysterious gardens of Aguedal.

Then we have our mules saddled, and, by the kind of grey avenue, climb towards the great gateway that since yesterday has attracted our eyes.

Passing at last under the high arch framed with arabesques and painted tiles we make our entry into Mekinez.

First of all, quagmires, ruins ; other ramparts, other enclosures, other gateways, dilapidated, demolished, pictures of the last desolation and antiquity. A few rare inhabitants, flattened in corners of walls, and clothed in burnouses of the same colour as the stones, watch us enter with expressions of vague mistrust.

The streets are wider, straighter than at Fez ; the aspect of the town more majestical, although even more dilapidated, more buried. Tall, grey mosques and immense minarets overlook the deserted squares. And on all the terraces, on all the cracked walls, on all the crownings of gates, grow tall weeds and wild flowers,

s

mignonette and Easter daisies, in tufted gardens or in hanging garlands; a veritable parterre of white and yellow flowers covers the whole of these ruins.

By little vaulted, down-sloping streets we are led to the house of the young pasha, there to deliver to him the Sultan's letter, which is the sesame giving us access to the town. In the approaches to his house, the walls are no longer decrepit, but covered with whitewash absolutely spotless, and the wild plants no longer embellish the roofs. A number of grave personages are seated there on stones, waiting for an audience; they are all draped in white woollen muslins, caught in by silken girdles, and veiling under-robes of blue or pink cloth.

The young pasha receives us at the threshold of his house. Murmuring a pious benediction, he first of all kisses the Sultan's seal on the letter we present to him; then he reads the letter and places himself at our disposal to lead us to the gardens of Aguedal, which he alone has the right to open. When would we like to repair thither? We reply: "At once," for we have no time to lose. And, on a sign, someone goes to fetch his horse.

Almost at once the horse is brought, at a gallop, held by two black slaves, restive and superb in the narrow little street where the hammering of its hoofs makes the chalk fly from the walls. It is white, with a long, trailing tail. The saddle and bridle, of water-green silk, are embroidered with gold.

Following the young pasha we plunge into the dead city, into the debris of Mekinez, which we have to traverse in its whole length, the palace and gardens of the Sultan being a considerable distance away, on the opposite side. The rare passers-by bow low before the young pasha, or approach and kiss the hem of his burnous.

More enclosures again, more formidable embattled ramparts, then open spaces, and ruins of which the plan is incomprehensible. Walls all sapped at the base, remaining upright one knows not how, but still imposing and grim, with their excessive proportions and high, crenellated bastions.

Towards the centre of the town we arrive before a wall higher even than all the others, infinitely high and long, the square bastions of which are aligned in diminishing perspective, like the " seven towers " of Stamboul. It encloses a town within the town, more walled and more impenetrable. There, we are on a kind of esplanade, from which one commands a view of the tranquilly mournful distances, of the succession of riven walls, of dead minarets

and empty terraces. Around us, however,
there are a few more people : men enveloped
in stone-coloured burnouses ; and a group of
unveiled Jewish women, in blue and red velvet
all spangled with gold, who look like extraordinary, gaily dressed dolls on the uniformity
of these neutral greys. And now, in the distance, issuing from the mouth of a deserted
street, we see some horsemen who seem worn
out by a long journey. They make signs to us,
call to us to stop, and hasten towards us.

Ah ! here are the presents, the presents
sent us by the Sultan ! Allah be praised !
We had ceased to expect them.

For the Governor of Algeria there is a superb
dappled-grey horse, which we are charged to
take to him ; and for us, an enormous locked
box, forming the load of a mule. We send the
horsemen back to our camp, outside the walls,
whither we shall shortly return to unpack these
precious things. But a crowd has gathered
round us, the news of these presents from
the sovereign has spread about the square,
and we are regarded now with respect as very
important chiefs.

Hereafter, long years hence, in the dim
future, when I shall see again in my home
these presents of the Caliph, who knows if I
shall remember to the end in how strange and

luminous a scene they one day appeared to
me, on this square of Mekinez, in front of
the empty palace of Mulai-Ismail, the Cruel
Sultan.

Directing our steps towards the gardens of
Aguedal, we continue to follow the mournful
grey wall, which points, above, its sharp
battlements into the blue sky. We are now in
another open square, the largest and most
central in Mekinez, surrounded by minarets
and old, windowless houses, coated in whitewash. And here, in the monotonous wall we
have followed for so long, a marvellous palace
gateway, all embroidered with mosaics, opens
as a surprise, attesting that this place, for all
its fearsome, prison-like aspects, was once the
resort of a magnificent sultan, as refined as an
artist in his rare luxury. And before this gate,
full in a great shaft of sunlight that falls and
outlines on the ground the black indentations
of the battlements, moves a group of unbelievable cavaliers, who look quite little on their
velvet-saddled horses, who laugh merrily in
childish voices, and whose burnouses, instead
of being white as is the custom for men, are of
all the known colours, the brightest and most
vivid. It is a troop of schoolboys who are
continuing the holiday of yesterday, of little
amins, little pashas, in brave costumes, mounted

on the state saddles of their fathers. It is a joyous cavalcade of children forming here amid the ruins, admirable of colour in this flood of sunshine, against the crushing and gloomy background of these palace walls. I think that this unexpected picture, surpassing even all the others, will remain in my eyes as the most Oriental that I have seen in all my journeyings in Al Moghreb.

And, behind these little people, what an astonishing and mysterious marvel is this palace gateway, opening in these immense ramparts! And the little people themselves, these schoolboys on horseback, how charming they are and how quaint-looking! Amongst them is a little fellow who can be no more than five or six years old. He is in a salmon-pink burnous, on a saddle of green velvet ; he rides a big horse that neighs and rears and tosses back into his face its white, ruffled mane ; and he has no fear, he smiles, rolling his bright eyes to right and left to see if he is being noticed. What a dear little chap he is, and what a horseman he will later on become !

This gate, which was that of Mulai-Ismail the Cruel, a contemporary of Louis XIV., is a gigantic ogive, supported on marble pillars and framed with exquisite festoons. All the adjacent wall, up to the battlements of the summit, is covered with mosaics of faience, as delicate and complicated as precious embroideries. The two square bastions that flank the gate on right and left are also covered with mosaics of a similar kind, and rest, too, on marble pillars. Roses, stars, endless minglings of intercepted lines, unimaginable geometrical combinations which baffle the eyes like some Chinese puzzle, but yet testify to a most cultivated and original taste, are accumulated there, in myriads of little pieces of glazed earth, sometimes in hollow, sometimes in relief, in such a way as to produce from a distance the illusion that elaborately figured stuffs, chatoyant, glistening, priceless, have been hung over these old stones in order to break a little the dreariness of the high ramparts. Yellow and gold are the predominant shades in these medleys of all colours; but the rain, the lapsing centuries, the baking sun, have set themselves to mingle these tints, to harmonise them, to give to the whole a warm and golden patina. Dark-coloured bands, like broad mourning ribbons, stretch horizontally, crossing and framing these gold and yellow embroideries: they are religious inscriptions, enscrolled Arabic characters, patiently executed in mosaics of black faience. And, along the upper band, a number of iron hooks, such as one sees on a butcher's stall, issue from the wall, to receive, on occasion, rows of human heads.

We continue on our way, still making for the gardens of Aguedal. Following the interminable wall, we encounter other mosaic gateways, other rows of bastions and battlements. More and more are we in regions abandoned, amid ruins. More open spaces, immense, deserted, surrounded by ramparts that look like the walls of destroyed cities; more, I know not how many more, dismantled gateways, broken arches, crumbling walls. And nowhere a soul; only the storks perched on the ruins and contemplating from above the surrounding desolation—an air of abandonment such as I have never seen before.

Then empty spaces, littered with rubbish and stones, broken by deep holes, caves, *oubliettes*. Cornfields, sometimes, between high imposing walls that once upon a time enclosed things so strictly hidden. Here and there, at the bottom of an enclosure into which we do not penetrate, appear, above the monotony of the battlemented ramparts, high, green-tiled roofs, embellished with moss and wild flowers: palaces of bygone sultans, the doors of which have been closed since the death of the master (for a new sultan must never inhabit the same dwelling as his predecessor), and which have been left to the slow destruction of the centuries.

And in all this chaotic debris, soon to know once more the torrid heat of the summer sun, there is always and everywhere the same exuberant profusion of herbs and flowers : veritable parterres of Easter daisies, anemones, red poppies, white poppies, pink poppies; immense natural gardens, exquisitely mournful.

Still we go on, led by the young pasha, trotting behind his horse caparisoned in green and gold. We know not now whether we are in the city or in the fields ; the boundary of the ruins is ill defined. Around us there are still great stretches of unfinished walls, that yet are near to falling with age : whims of successive sovereigns who disappeared into the eternal abysm before they could complete the work they had begun. Long lines of embattled ramparts stretch into the distances of the deserted campaign, to disappear one knows not where, amid thickets and herbage.

.   .   .   .

The gardens of Aguedal! How desolate a spot! What an aspect of unexpected mournfulness—even after all the melancholy things our eyes have grown accustomed to seeing here ! First, a door warped and worm-eaten, which opens with a secretive air at the end of a path-

way overgrown with weeds. At the summons
of the pasha, a white-bearded guardian draws
back the inner bolts and shuts them again
behind us when we have passed. A first
enclosure, a kind of courtyard of death, still
between these walls at least fifty feet high ;
then a second door bolted with iron ; a second
enclosure, another door again—and at last the
" gardens " are before us. We stand dum-
foundered before the bare immensity of a kind
of endless prairie of short grass sprinkled with
daisies. Herds of cattle and horses are grazing
there in the wild state ; in the distance, bands
of ostriches move about ; and all around are
bones, empty carcasses, littering the ground.
Gardens there are none ; a few poor trees
beyond, in an old enclosure forming a kind of
orchard ; otherwise nothing but this mournful,
immured prairie, which yet is so extensive that
its grey wall is scarcely visible in the distance,
seems no more than a line bounding the plain
on which these herds are scattered. The
country beyond, absolutely solitary, is green
beneath a gloomy sky ; it might be a landscape
of some country of the north, in a region without
villages and without roads, some manor park in
a deserted land. The horses, the cattle, the
little white daisies, they, too, recall our climate,
and here and there are pools of water in which

croak the most ordinary frogs. The unfamiliar thing, that which strikes the sole discordant, exotic note, is the Arab chief, at our side—he, and these ostriches, moving about as if at home, on their long, slender legs. If the place is mournful, at least it is not commonplace ; for very few Europeans can ever have penetrated into these " gardens " of the Sultan.

Our mules step with a certain hesitation ; they are shy of these dead carcasses lying in the grass. Farther on they draw back before a band of ostriches, which advance to look at us, stretching out their long, bald necks, and then turn tail and make off, waddling on their long legs.

We are curious to know what may have become of three Norman mares presented to Mulai-Hassan by the French Government, some four years ago, on the occasion of a previous mission, and we try to find them amongst the number of horses that are here.

At length we recognise them, grouped close together, separated from their kind and forming, visibly, a band apart. Each of them has its little foal, son of a foreign sire—and we are not a little astonished to see these beasts, at the end of four years, still mindful of their common origin, living thus together, as if aware of their exile.

Then we follow the enclosure walls, in order to visit three or four ancient buildings that back upon them, wide distances apart. They are the garden kiosks, surrounded by black cypresses. They have verandahs looking on to Aguedal, and supported by charming old colonnades. Abandoned, perhaps for centuries, they look woefully forlorn, under the accumulated layers of whitewash which conceal their arabesques. Their doors are bolted, condemned, even filled up with stones. Formerly, no doubt, the sultanas, the cloistered and invisible beauties, used often to come and sit in front of these kiosks, under these columns, to beguile themselves with thoughts of liberty in contemplating the distances of these prairies of daisies. And mysterious dramas of love must have come to pass here, that will never be written.

On leaving the gardens of Aguedal, the young pasha leads us back by different ways, through inner dependencies of the palace, but always between the gigantic battlemented walls, which, in their excessive height, give to all this place its character of grim impenetrability. The courts, the avenues, the open spaces, are always empty and dead. The prevailing colour of all these walls, of all these ruins, is an earthy yellow, streaked with reddish-brown.

The chalk used at Mekinez is generally mixed with ochre; and moreover, and more especially, the years, the rain, the sun, the lichen, have endued everything with the primitive colours of the rocks and soil. These dependencies of the palace are immense; in valleys, coursed by streams, we traverse uncultivated orchards, which are delightful medleys of orange-trees, pomegranate-trees, fig-trees and willows. The fair captive sultanas have the wherewithal to lose themselves amid the verdure and can enjoy the illusion of being in woodlands wild.

In all the fissures in the walls grow nopal cacti, as large as trees, which outspread in the sunshine their yellow flowers and bluish, rigid, racket-like leaves. And a number of storks, motionless on one leg on the summit of the battlements, look down upon us from above.

The young pasha takes us to see a stretch of artificial water, destined to serve as a bathing-place for the ladies of the harem. On it, too, the Sultan purposes to sail the electric launch that we have brought him. It is a square lake some three or four hundred yards in length. On three of its sides it is surrounded by a sinister embattled wall sixty feet high, which is re-flected upside down in the still water, giving a false impression of depth. The fourth side communicates, by a quay paved with flagstones, with the great empty esplanade leading to the palace. It is on this esplanade we walk, still absolutely alone, our eyes embracing on all sides rows of formidable ramparts that succeed one another, cross one another, enclose one another—and enclose us. Above these old broken walls upon which the devouring noontide sun now falls, appear once more the weed-covered roofs of the palaces of ancient sultans —which still shelter, perhaps, marvellous, un-dreamt-of debris—and beyond, the more distant medley of terraces, mosques, minarets, and cracked and crumbling walls : all the solemn desolation of Mekinez, upraised against the mournful sky. A music of grasshoppers rises from the old stones ; and the whole surface of the immured lake is pinked with little black dots which are the heads of frogs croaking with all their might in the silence of the ruins.

One single new building appears beyond, above the old walls : it is the palace of the present Sultan, white as snow, with a roof of green tiles and blue penthouses. The Sultan spends scarcely a month there each year, obliged as he is to remain longer at Fez and Morocco, his two other capitals ; but this palace is inhabited at the present moment by a detachment of ladies of the harem who left Fez last week—and who, needless to say, were carefully sequestrated behind a multitude of walls before our arrival in the gardens.

As we turn away to depart a group of black washerwomen, wearing large silver rings in their ears, issue from the palace with bundles of linen on their heads : the underclothing of the invisible fair ones, which they begin nonchalantly to wash in the lake, singing native songs the while.

I know not how many enclosures we have to pass on our way out, nor how many gateways, nor how many turnings we have to take, between enormous ramparts calcined by the sun and interspersed with cacti.

It turns out that we are about to leave by that same marvellous mosaic gateway of Mulai-Ismail which we admired this morning. We pass under its ogive, in its shadow, between its marble pillars, and now we are outside, in the bright sunshine, in the central square of the town. Some groups of Arabs loitering there, perceiving their pasha between us, approach and bow low, almost prostrating themselves. Formerly, the informal morning outgoings of Mulai-Ismail must have been something in this kind.

.   .   .   .

In this square we thank the pasha and bid him good-bye—to make our way to the Jewish town, there to pay the promised visit to our friend of yesterday evening. That will be a change to us from all these dead grandeurs.

To reach this Jewish town we have to traverse quarters more inhabited. First that of the merchants of trinkets and jewels, where on the two sides of the street, in little box-shaped booths, quaint displays of silver and coral shine on old counters of rough wood. And then a quite unique street, long and straight and wide as a boulevard, bordered by roofless houses, like cubes of stone. It rises towards a hill on the top of which a saint's tomb outlines on the crude blue of the sky its painted cupola, flanked by two tall slender palms.

At the end of this street opens the gate of the Jews. And, as soon as this gate is passed, the aspect of things suddenly changes; it is as if one had been transported, without transition, into another country. In place of the immobility and silence is a compact swarming; in place of brown-visaged men, slow and majestic of carriage, draped in white wool, there are here pale and fresh-complexioned men, in long ringlets and black skull-caps, who walk with head bent down, closely wrapped in dark and scanty robes; and unveiled women, very pale, with lightly marked eyebrows; and a number of young Hebrews, fresh-looking, pink and

white, effeminate, with crafty, timorous expressions. A population over-dense, stifling in
this narrow quarter, out of which the Sultan
does not permit it to live. Little streets
encumbered with traders, and on the ground
all sorts of debris, pickings, refuse ; a general
dirtiness, arising out of the accumulation, that
astonishes, even after that of the Arab streets;
and evil odours without a name, at once acrid
and stale, that nearly choke one.

Our friend of yesterday evening comes to
meet us, advised no doubt by the noise of the
crowd greeting our arrival. He has still the
same pleasant, kindly face, but to-day, for a
millionaire, he is very poorly clad : a faded
robe, unrelieved, colourless, nondescript. It
is the custom, it seems, for the rich Jews to
affect in the street these unpretentious airs.

The door of his house is very modest also,
very little and very low, by the side of a stream
charged with refuse.

But, within, we stand astonished before a
strange luxury, before a group of women
covered in gold and precious stones, who receive
us with smiles, amid a scene of " The Thousand
and One Nights."

We are in an interior court, open to the sky,
with, all around, a colonnade and denticulated
arches. Glistening mosaics cover the ground

T

and the walls up to the height of a man ; above begin the infinitely varied arabesques, the marvellous filigree-work of stone, set off with blue and green and red and gold. The patient artists who decorated this house are the descendants of those who carved the palaces of Granada, and they have changed nothing, during so many centuries, in the artistic traditions bequeathed to them by their fathers ; the same fairylike embroideries that one admires in the Alhambra under a coating of dust are revealed here in all the splendour of their bright freshness.

The women that are in this court—they are dazzling in the sunshine—have petticoats of velvet embroidered with gold, chemises of silk laminated with gold, open bodices almost entirely covered with gold. On their arms, in their ears, on their ankles, they wear heavy rings studded with precious stones ; and their pointed caps, their kinds of little helmets, are made of brilliantly coloured silks figured with gold. Their faces are pale, with a waxlike pallor, their dark eyes are darkly encircled ; and their fillets *à la juive*, black as the feathers of crows, hang quite flat along their cheeks.

The mistress of the house is the only one in the group that is not absolutely young. The others, who are presented to us as married women, and must be so in fact if one may judge from the luxury of their attire, are children of about ten years of age. (Amongst the Jews of Fez and Mekinez it is the custom for girls to marry at ten years of age and boys at fourteen.)

All these little fairies shake hands with us, smiling graciously. The welcome of the mistress of the house is cordial, and even distinguished. She is the most sumptuously dressed of all; her crimson velvet petticoat, her sky-blue velvet bodice disappear under embossed figurings of gold, and her earrings are threaded with fine pearls and emeralds as large as nuts.

We had never before seen the inside of the house of a rich Jew, and this unexpected and unimagined luxury seems to us a dream, after the sordid meanness and evil odours of the street.

We decline to partake of luncheon, despite the insistence of our hosts ; but our reception seems to afford so sincere a pleasure that, to avoid causing pain, we consent to accept a cup of tea.

It is on the first storey that this tea is to be served to us. We ascend a narrow and very steep staircase of mosaics, followed by all the little women in their costumes of idols. We cross an upper gallery, festooned, open to the air, and gilded ; and enter a hall decorated in the style of the Alhambra, there to sit down on the floor on velvet cushions and wonderful rugs.

On the floor, too, our spiced tea smokes in silver tea urns and samovars of great richness.

The windows of this hall are little trefoils and little roses cut out in a great variety of forms. On the walls are those same mosaics, that same sculptured filigree-work of which the Arabs have the inimitable secret. And the ceiling is a series of little cupolas, of little starry domes, for which the rarest and most difficult geometrical combinations seem to have been exhausted, as well as the most extraordinary minglings of colours.

Through the delicate carvings of the stained-glass windows enter blue and yellow and red rays, which fall at hazard on the silks, on the golds, on the brilliant costumes of the women. And, in the midst of us, in a silver brasier, burns the precious wood of India, spreading a cloud of odorous smoke.

After the three cups of tea prescribed by custom, after the " gazelles' hoofs," the water-melon jam, the sweetmeats of every sort, we make a decided attempt to take our leave, to depart. But our host renews his invitation to luncheon with so insistent an entreaty that, tired of saying no, we say yes. Thereupon an expression of sincere pleasure overspreads his face and all the little married ladies give a little leap of joy.

Before sitting down to the luncheon, however, we must needs be shown over the house, of which our host seems justly proud.

First the terraces—in other words, the roofs —which form the customary promenade of the family. One scarcely dares to walk upon them, so spotless and snowy is the chalk with which they are covered. They are divided into different parts, each affording a different aspect of the desolate grandeur of roundabout. And there are such entanglements in this town, where, for centuries, buildings have been reared against and crowded upon ruins, that one part of these white terraces thrusts itself under the gloomy formidable archway of a crumbling fortress, built there formerly by Mulai-Ismail, the Cruel Sultan. From these high promenades one dominates first of all the Jewish quarter, with its airless houses, close-set, heaped one upon another as by some force of compression, and its sickening odours. Farther on, the rest of Mekinez, all the incomprehensible unfolding of great fortress and palace walls, to which, by contrast, space and extent have

been given without stint; and, in the middle
of the grimmest and highest of these walls, the
marvellous gateway by which, an hour or so ago,
we issued from the seraglios, the great mosaic-
embroidered ogive that was the entrance of
honour of the glorious Sultan; and farther on
again, beyond all these ramparts and ruins,
glimpses of the wild countryside, where the
brigands make the law. " It has happened,"
our host tells us, " at certain times when the
Sultan and his army have been on expeditions
in the south, it has happened that the gates of
Mekinez have had to be shut in broad daylight,
so bold and dangerous did the marauding Zemur
become." All the Israelite family has climbed
with us, one after another, up the steep and
narrow staircase, in order to do us the honours
of this open-air place. The velvet and gold
costumes of the women stand out sharply against
the brilliant whiteness of the terraces; the little
married ladies all are here. I notice particu-
larly two little sisters-in-law, about ten years
old, who stand arm-in-arm, and look very
charming and very quaint, with their too
enlarged and too darkly ringed eyes, which
already seem to have ceased to be the eyes of
children. The magnificent bracelets that encircle their wrists and ankles—they are wedding
presents and will serve them later on, when they

are grown up—are now too large for their childish limbs and are held in place by ribbons. And with them all, young or not, what one sees of hair, under the little helmet of golden net, is an imitation in silk ; two fillets of black silk, sedulously combed and faultlessly in place, frame their wax-white cheeks ; and two little curls, also of black silk, hang loose like paint-brushes over their delicate ears. As for their real hair, it is invisible, hidden I know not where.

As my eyes wander over these terraces, to the melancholy horizon before which these women are born and die, I realise, for a moment, with a kind of horror, what the life of these Israelites must be, bound fearfully to the observances of the laws of Moses, and immured within this narrow quarter, in the midst of this mummified city, separated from all the rest of the world.

One of the glories of the house is its garden, a garden that makes us smile. It measures five or six yards square, maybe, and its high walls are painted with yoke-elm; in it grow a few poor starveling orange-trees. But, seeing how precious space is, one must needs be very rich to possess a garden in this quarter. The present Sultan, our host tells us, is very well disposed to the Jews. He has promised, when next he stays in Mekinez, to have a new town built for them. And so they hope soon to have more room and to be better able to breathe.

The whole house is furnished and decorated in the most exquisite Arab taste, and you might imagine that you were in the house of some fashionable vizier, if the proportions were not so small, and if, above all, you did not see in each apartment, framed under glass, the Tables of the Law, or Hebraic inscriptions, or the sombre countenance of Moses, or some other indication of that particular kind of obscurity which is not the Mussulman obscurity.

.   .   .   .

Our luncheon is ready. It is served on the ground floor, in a hall opening on to the great court, all in filigree-work of stone embellished with gold. The interior walls are decorated with mosaics of exquisite delicacy, representing rows of Moorish arches, within which are strangely complicated rose designs like the figurings of the kaleidoscope. The ceiling is composed of those innumerable little pendentives, joined one to another, which I can only compare with the crystals of hoarfrost suspended from the branches of trees in winter.

Out of compliment to us, the table is laid in the European manner, on a white cloth. The china-ware is French, from Limoges, of Empire style, with gilt bands. At the end of what odyssies have these things come to be stranded at Mekinez ?

Four musicians are brought in, two vocalists, a violin and a drum. They sit down on the ground, at our feet, and begin to play, without a pause, rapid, strident, mournful things. Our hostess, for all her pearls and emeralds, chooses to superintend the cooking and to wait upon us herself ; all of which she does, too, with a perfect good grace and a distinction all her own.

Some twenty different courses follow one after another, washed down by two or three varieties of an old and quite palatable red wine, which the Jews cultivate on the hillsides around Mekinez. And while the music rages on the ground, while the smoke of the Indian wood, which is burning before us, veils our luncheon with an odorous blue cloud, we see, in the beautiful luminous court, the family group in its gold-bedizened costumes, and our eyes are attracted once more to the two little sisters-in-law, as they pass and pass again, arm-in-arm, their childish antics contrasting with their heavy jewellery and their garb of great ladies.

.   .   .   .

When the time comes for us to depart we know not how to thank these good people, whom we shall never see anywhere again, and to whom we should like to offer hospitality in our turn, if, by some extraordinary chance, they were to visit our country.

Out in the sordid street once more we find a considerable mob, which has gathered there in the curious expectation of seeing us; all the quarter is out of doors, and we proceed through a compact crowd until the moment when, the gate of the Jews passed, we relapse into the solitude of the Arab town.

The overpowering two o'clock sun blazes on the tranquillities of the ruins, where thousands of grasshoppers are chirping. We issue from the enclosures of the great ramparts, and begin to descend towards our camp.

Awaiting us there are the horsemen who brought our presents from Fez. Before dismissing them we think it well to verify the contents of our cases, for fear they may have been plundered during the night of the journey; and, on the announcement of the unpacking, our muleteers make a close circle round us, with eyes avid to see. The men of a little caravan that has encamped near us in our absence draw near also, greatly attracted by the spectacle; and there are soon some thirty Arabs, suspicious of movement and draped in majestic rags, who closely encompass us, in the solitariness of this

cemetery, mute from impatience, with the idea
of admiring the presents of the Caliph. We
open the first box : it is the green velvet saddle,
very sumptuously embroidered with gold,
which we are charged to take to the Governor
of Algeria, at the same time as his dappled
horse ; murmurs of passionate admiration
greet its appearance in the sun.

And now let us unpack the prodigiously long
box which presumably contains our personal
presents. For each of us, a Souss gun in its
red case ; an ancient gun, five feet in length,
entirely covered with silver. For each of us,
also, a Moroccan pasha's sabre, in an inlaid
scabbard, with a strap of silk and gold ; the
handle of rhinoceros horn, the blade and hilt
damascened in gold. It gleams in the warm
light of the sun, and exclamations of the most
excited kind escape from our entourage. In
his enthusiasm for the Caliph who is able to
make such desirable presents, a camel-driver
goes so far as to cry : " Allah render victorious
our Sultan Mulai-Hassan ! Allah prolong his
days, *even at the cost of my own life !* "

And we begin to think we have been
imprudent in awakening around us such
covetousness.

.   .   .   .

We ascend once more towards the holy city,

seated on our mules and preceded by the old kaid in charge. This time, it is to wander at hazard and in quest of rugs and arms until sunset.

The bazaar, much smaller, darker and more mournful than that of Fez, is completely empty when we arrive. Along the walls all the little shutters of the merchants' niches are pulled down and closed. It is explained to us that everybody is at the mosque ; in a few moments they will be back again. We had not realised that it is half-past three, the hour of the fourth prayer of the day.

By degrees, one after another, the merchants return, with slow steps, draped in their transparent muslins, quite white in the gloom of these little vaulted streets. Absorbed in their dream, careless or disdainful of our presence, they raise the shutters of their niches and, climbing, seat themselves within, their beads in their hands, without looking at us. Yet we are the only buyers—and one is tempted to ask what purpose is served by a bazaar in this necropolis. There are on sale burnouses, costumes, figured leather, numbers of stirrups inlaid with silver or gold ; and some of those coverlets of barbarous designs, woven in the south by the women of the tribes, of evenings at the mouth of the tents, amongst the Beni-M'guil and the Tuaregs.

We wander for a long time amongst these deserted and mournful quarters. We pass, always in the obscurity of these vaulted streets, before many immense mosques, where, by furtive glances, we get glimpses of mysterious lines of arches and columns. Then we reach the quarter, a little less dead, of the jewel merchants.

And what strange old jewels they are that are sold at Mekinez! In what epochs can they ever have been new? There is not one but has an air of extreme antiquity: old rings for wrist or ankle, polished by age-long rubbing against human skin; large clasps for fastening the veils; old little silver bottles with coral pendants, to hold the black for painting the eyes, with hooks by which to attach them to the waistband; boxes for Korans, all engraved with arabesques and bearing the seal of Solomon; old necklaces of sequins worn smooth by the necks of women dead—and a quantity of those large trefoils, of beaten silver enchasing a green stone, which are worn on the breast as a talisman against the evil eye. In the niches of the old walls, in front of the sellers sitting cross-legged, these things are displayed on little counters of dirty and worm-eaten wood.

We are near the quarter of the Jews; many from amongst them, espying us, approach and surround us, offering us jewels again, bracelets, extraordinary old rings, and emerald earrings, all which things they produce, with airs of mystery, from the pockets of their black robes, having first cast distrustful glances around.

Come also the sellers of Rabat carpets; carpets of fine wool, which they spread out on the ground, in the dust, on the rubbish and bones, to show us the rare designs and the brilliant colours.

.   .   .   .

The sun is sinking and begins to cast its rays in long golden bands over the ruins. We therefore bring our laboriously haggled purchases to an end, and leaving the holy city, which we shall never see again, make our way to our tents.

Before passing the last enclosure wall, however, we come to a stop at a sort of little bazaar which previously we had not noticed. It is that of the merchants of bric-à-brac, and goodness knows what quaint old odds and ends shops of the kind may contain in Mekinez.

These old curiosity shops, if one may call them so, are huddled near a gate opening on to the deserted country, at the foot of the high, frowning ramparts and in the shade of some century-old mulberry-trees which at this moment are decked in their tender green foliage

of April. It is old arms above all else that one
finds here : rusty yataghans, long Souss guns;
and old leather amulets for the hunt and
war; ridiculous-looking powder-horns, and also
musical instruments : snake-skin guitars, bagpipes and tabours. By analogy, no doubt,
with the debris that they sell, the merchants
are nearly all old men, decrepit, bent, done for.

Some beggars, who have found a lodging in
holes of stone at this entrance to the city, assist
in our purchases : a one-armed fellow covered
with sores; a mangy cripple; and a number of
those men whose means of sight consist of two
bloody holes about which the flies congregate ;
old robbers these, whose eyes, in accordance
with the law, have been put out with red-hot
iron.

The traders in this bazaar are very poor no
doubt, they are in sad need of sales, for they
busy themselves with us, they surround us.
We make many surprising acquisitions for next
to nothing. The yellow hour of sunset, bringing
with it a sudden chill, finds us still there, near
this desolate gate and under the branches of
these old trees, ringed by some fifty wild figures
in rags, Berbers, Arabs and Soudanese.

.   .   .   .

It is known in the town that we are leaving
to-morrow morning at daybreak. Accordingly,

as soon as we are back in our tents, some Jews make their way down to the camp, to renew their offers of feathers, ostrich eggs, more silver jewels, more Rabat carpets. As long as the twilight lasts, they continue obstinately to display these things before us, on the grass-grown tombs.

Later on the young pasha comes on horseback to bid us good-bye. Then the night guard arrives, and, last of all, with lanterns, the cortège of our pompous *mouna*. Then, for our guards, begins the great nocturnal orgy of chickens and sheep and couscous.

CHAPTER XXXIV

30th April.

IN the first magnificent rays of the sun we strike camp, leaving the remnants of our feast to the dogs and vultures.

Very quickly the holy city disappears behind us, masked by wild hills.

Mountain passes, carpets of flowers. Large pink bindweed amid the bluish aloes; but bindweed in such profusion that it looks as if large handfuls of pink ribbons had been flung amongst the pale, ash-coloured leaves of the aloes. And so it is for miles. Then come uniform zones of blue bindweed, but so blue that from a distance you would think you saw pools of water reflecting the beautiful deep colour of the sky.

Not till to-morrow do we pick up the road to Tangier which we followed with the embassy on our way out. To-day we are crossing a region even less frequented, and to us unknown—a region that is a desert indeed. It is warmer than on the outward journey; the scent of Africa is more pronounced in the country, and there is an even greater abundance of flowers, a greater concert of the vibrant music of insects, in a greater silence.

We are making rather forced marches, forty miles a day about. Our camping grounds, discussed and fixed beforehand with the kaid who leads us, are spaced on that basis; and this evening we hope to pitch our camp beyond these spurs of the Atlas, at the entrance to the endless plain where the Sebu winds.

This time our manner of travelling is very different, and the country, which before we traversed in state, in the midst of the horsemen of the tribes assembled from afar in our honour, now appears to us in its true aspect, in its mournful tranquillity, with its great empty expanses. With all respect to our companions left behind at Fez—of whom we cherish the most cordial recollections—we prefer to return thus, like ordinary worthy Moroccans, not attracting the curiosity of passing caravans, not even making now a blot on the solitude through which we pass, disguised as we are in our burnouses, and all bronzed by the sun. We feel ten times more in Africa, chatting to our muleteers, listening to their songs and stories, initiated into a thousand aspects, a thousand little details of an intimate Morocco, which we had not suspected on the pompous outward journey.

The old kaid who intrigued for the honour and profit of leading us back to Tangier is an inhabitant of Mekinez, where, it seems, he possesses a harem of young white wives, and he had asked us yesterday for permission to pass the night in his home. This morning, at daybreak, he is back in the camp, true to his instructions. But to-day, straight as ever on his beast, he looks like a corpse dried up by the sun and, instead of leading the march, he lags wearily behind, A black muleteer, who is the buffoon of our company, regarding him with an untranslatable wink, gives this explanation of his fatigue : " He slept last night in a *silo*." It is impossible to render in English the mocking intention of the phrase, or the inimitable, monkey-like drollery with which this nigger uttered it. Nevertheless the old kaid moves us to a real pity in his fight against old age. Too proud to admit that he is tired he spurs his horse with a heart-breaking vexation each time we show signs of slowing down to wait for him.

Throughout the day we encounter not a village, nor a house, nor any sign of cultivation; only, at wide intervals, some *douars* of nomads, installed generally at a great distance from the track ; but the watch-dogs scent us nevertheless, and howl in the silent campaign as we pass. Their tents, yellowish, brownish,

are pitched always in circles—as grow toad-
stools, which they resemble ; the herds graze
in the middle, and, by the side of each *douar*,
there are in the prairie two or three large, de-
nuded, bare and dirty rounds—which are the
sites of old encampments abandoned after the
exhaustion of the herbage. We are told that
these tents to-day are inhabited only by
women, all the able-bodied men having been
requisitioned by the Pasha of Mekinez for
his expedition against the Zemur.

About midday, at the crossing of a ford, we
meet a travelling Berber tribe, their clothes
tucked up very high in the running water. In
accordance with the Berber custom, the women
are but very partially veiled, and some of the
more youthful amongst them are decidedly
pretty. The herds cross with them, bellowing,
bleating, pursued and harassed by very busy
dogs. Some of the little girls have lambs in
their arms, and from one of those large baskets,
called *chouari*, which the mules carry on their
back, appears the astonished head of a little
baby foal which has been put to bed there and
seems to be very comfortable.

·　　·　　·　　·　　·　　·　　·

At length, at about four o'clock, from the
height of the last mountain of the chain of the
Atlas, we see the plain of the Sebu, which we

have to cross to-morrow, looking like a luminous
sea. In the foreground it is all marbled,
streaked, with yellow, rose and violet, according
to its zones of flowers which men have never
disturbed. But in the distance, towards the
clean circle of the horizon, all these gaudy
colourings are blurred, melt into a uniform
blue, like that of the sea itself.

We descend a steep slope, and, after another
hour's march, pitch our camp in the plain,
beyond the foot of the mountains, near the holy
tomb of Sidi-Kassem, and by the side of a
cluster of stubble huts which that marabout
protects.

It is always a delightful hour when, the camp
pitched, the day's long journey done, one sits
voluptuously before one's tent, on a bed of
wild sweet flowers that are always different,
always new. All around is immense space;
the air smells good; it is impregnated with that
same scent as it has with us, though in a less
degree and in more fleeting kind, at the time
of haymaking; the Arab clothes are free and
light, augmenting the sensation of repose that
one experiences, outstretched there, under the
cool evening sky, and the profound clearness
that is everywhere about, making a feast for
the eyes, it seems also that one breathes it,
that one tastes the physical impression of it

in filling the lungs with air. After those long hours rocked by the incessant little jolts of the motion of the mule, the immobility of this old Arab earth on which one is about to sleep seems infinitely restful; and then the sense of appetite is keen, and the thoughts turn longingly to the approaching hour of couscous, even to those barbarous cookings that the muleteers are preparing hard by: the sheep and chickens roasted in the grass.

We are here close to the Beni-Hassem, whose territory we are going to cross to-morrow at a single stretch in order to put the river Sebu between them and our next encampment; the Zemur too are not far away; but it is hard to conceive of danger in a spot so peaceful and so decked with flowers.

To the little village at our side the flocks come bleating home, brought in by hooded children. Shortly afterwards some milk is brought to us, still warm, in earthen bowls; and the old chief who is to provide us with a guard for the night comes and talks with us.

After exchanging a few conventional questions, we inquire about the three brigands who were captured here on the day of our previous passing. "Ah!" he says, "the three brigands? This is the fifth or sixth day they have had the salt in their hands."

Oh, the unhappy wretches ! We feared as much, but the fact of it makes us shudder none the less. And so these men, who were in this plain at the same time as we, breathing this same pure air, free as ourselves to course about, having like us health, space, have been for five or six days, for five or six nights, awaiting death, their nails bent forward into the cloven flesh, pressed tight, tight, by a horrible glove that will never be removed ; with nothing to hope for, no alleviation, no commiseration, for the law requires that the suffering should go on in a continuous augmentation, and that they should die at last by the very excess of their agony. And our high-strung European nerves are set on edge, and the evening's peace, in the blurred hour of the approach of sleep, is troubled by the picture of these three tortured malefactors.

CHAPTER XXXV

1st May.

THERE has been firing all through the night, around the camp, in our ears. It was our guards, very apprehensive, very restless. We heard them saying to one another: "It's a thief! No, it's a jackal!" And they disputed about the shapes of what they thought they saw approaching in the dark: "They were men, I tell you, but men walking on all-fours, crouching, crouching low."

.   .   .   .

At half-past four, in the pale morning twilight, they awaken us, in accordance with instructions, in order that we may strike camp and resume our journey. For we want to cross the Sebu before nightfall, leaving behind us this territory of the Beni-Hassem.

And awakened thus in one's little canvas house—which is always alike, with mats and carpets arranged always in the self-same fashion —it frequently happens that one has no longer a clear recollection of the appearance of the surrounding country, which, on the contrary, is always changing; now a great dead city, now a desolate plain, now an overlooking mountain.

As I emerge from my tent this morning, my mind still sluggish with sleep, I have before me an infinite expanse, covered with violet lucerne and pink mallows, beneath a sky entirely black; an unimaginable profusion of flowers in a flat and boundless solitude, resembling at once a Garden of Eden and a desert. It is scarcely yet enlightened, and the thick clouds, which seem to weigh upon the herbage, make the vault of the sky darker than the earth beneath. But presently, at the edge of the plain, in the lowest part of the tenebrous sky, the yellowish sun reveals its presence by long rays which it casts all at once across the vast intensity of shadow in which we are; we divine it without seeing it, and, by contrast with these luminous rays that emanate from it, the surrounding darkness seems suddenly to thicken. This mysterious sunrise reminds me strongly of those which were once familiar to me on the coasts of Brittany, and on the northern seas in times of mist. But while I am watching, disorientated, wondering, this distant breaking forth of pale light, some large beasts pass, one after another, before the sun; slow-moving, rocking beasts, whose long legs project interminable shadows on the plain: the caravans of Africa! Then I recover the notion of my whereabouts, which I had three-parts lost.

The clouds disperse, disappear one knows not where. On all sides at once the blue re-appears and settles uniformly over the entire dome of the sky.

Seven hours' travelling, without a halt, across the plain, amid the magnificence of Easter daisies, marigolds, lucerne and mallows, passing from time to time files of camels and heavily laden donkeys, all that comes and goes between Tangier and Fez—between Europe and the Soudan. At last we grow tired of this pro-fusion of flowers, of the sameness of the flowers, seen in the semi-somnolence induced by the jogging motion of the mules and made heavy by the burning sun.

At about two o'clock in the afternoon we make a halt for an hour at a chance spot, of which this picture remains to me : the inevit-able plain, boundless, flowered as never was any garden ; and alone, apart, the old spent kaid, on his knees at prayer. It is in a zone of white Easter daisies flecked with rose-coloured poppies. The old man nigh to death, his face earth-coloured, his beard like a white lichen, clothed in the same fresh colours as the poppies and Easter daisies amid which he kneels, his long white veils half-revealing his caftan of pink cloth ; his horse, white, with a red, high-peaked saddle, grazing by his side, its head plunged in the herbage ; himself half buried in the flowers, in the white and pink flowers, in the midst of the immense plain of flowers infinitely deserted under the profound blue of the summer sky ; prostrated on this earth which soon will cover him, imploring the mercy of Allah with that fervour of prayer which comes from the presentiment of approaching nothingness.

. . . .

We cross the Sebu at four o'clock and encamp near a village of the Beni-Malek, on the north bank of the river.

CHAPTER XXXVI

2nd May.

OUR little troop is swelled by some new recruits : chance Arabs encountered by the way, solitary travellers who have asked to be allowed to join us, for fear of robbers. We have also two of those individuals called rakkas, who form an important corporation at Fez under the direction of an amin, and whose business it is to carry letters across Morocco, running night and day if needs be, according to the price that is paid for their services, safe to sleep afterwards for a week on end.

In the fresh morning we traverse for some four hours those sandy solitudes carpeted with bracken and little rare flowers which we know already, but which seem to us quite different, more mournful, more melancholy, vaster even, now that we travel in their midst alone, without the noisy escort of the embassy, which used to fire its guns to windward. The air no longer smells of powder, is no longer agitated by the whirlwind passage of the fantasias, and is tranquil, pure, vivifying and sweet. And the light is wonderful. Beyond the immense sweep of the plain, the mountains into which we shall enter to-morrow are outlined as by a clean, firm pencilling, in colours frankly intense, on a limpid void which is the sky. From time to time a stork watches us file past, motionless on its stilt-like legs, or perhaps passes in the air, beating above our heads its great black and white wings. And that is all that animates this deserted country in which one feels so abundantly alive.

.   .   .   .

About midday, amid hills violet with lavender, the penetrating scent of which is augmented by the heat of the sun, we perceive a little ravine-like hollow, in which by chance there is a tree, a real, large tree, an old wild fig-tree, gnarled like a banian of India. And it is so tempting, so extraordinary in this bare country, where there is no shade but that of errant clouds, that we dismount in order to descend into the hollow and make our midday halt there. The place, select and rare, is already occupied by a half-score of bullocks, huddled close together, almost hidden by the thick large leaves, thrice happy in this moist coolness, when all radiates and burns around. But they give place to us without contest, running away fearstruck at our approach, and we install ourselves as masters in the little oasis.

This fig-tree must be several hundred years old, so thick are its branches and so extraordinarily twisted. A stream flows at its foot, murmuring over black pebbles, amid watercresses, blue forget-me-nots, all those water plants known since childhood in the streams of our French countrysides. And, behind the bushy mass of the tree, an overhanging rock projects in the form of the vault of a cave, making as it were a second little room, more covered still and more private, which is carpeted with maiden-hair, and from which a spring trickles. In entering it one has a delicious sensation of coolness and shade, after the oppression of the burning light which floods the hills of lavender outside. Among the roots of the fig-tree, as in an arm-chair, we stretch ourselves idly, our bare feet in the water of the stream. In all that surrounds us there is nothing African, nothing foreign; it seems to us that we are in some corner of a wild France, of a France of olden time, in the cloudless noontide of a resplendent June. And the animals here, which have never been troubled by man, have no fear of us; slowly, very slowly, from amongst the reeds, the tortoises bring near their black carapaces to eat the crumbs of bread that we let fall; and the green tree-frogs light upon us, let us handle them, stroke them.

Of all the shady spots, of all the cool streams on the banks of which I have come to rest, at burning noontides, in the course of so many diverse expeditions, amid circumstances so different, in various countries of the world, I do not think that any has brought me a more penetrating impression of peace than this, with a more intimate desire to bury myself in the green peacefulness of nature.

.   .   .   .

At the close of this same day, the second of our month of May, and the first of the Arab month of Ramadan, we encamp before Czar-el-Kebir.

And in the evening our kaid and our muleteers, who this morning began to observe the fast ordained by the Koran for the whole of this month, are all standing, watching the town behind which the sun is setting, awaiting with impatience the hour when the white flags of the prayer shall be hoisted on the mosques, the hour of the holy Moghreb, after which it will be permissible for them to eat and drink.

The sky is absolutely yellow, of a pale lemon-yellow; an intense yellow light is spread all about; and against this clear sunset the town is outlined in sharp silhouette: its heavy minarets in black; all its embattled walls, with their swathings of chalk, in a kind of grey-blue, cold and dead; in black also its few tall palms, on stems as slender as threads, which here and there droop their bouquets of plumes above the house-tops. And in the luminous yellow of the background, overlooking all, the new moon of Ramadan shows its slim crescent like the mark of a thumbnail that had come to shine. It is a setting ideally Arab, lighted with a supreme art.

"Allah Akbar!" The holy hour sounds at last, the immense cry re-echoes over the town; on your knees, all ye woollen burnouses : it is the Moghreb, the first Moghreb of Ramadan.

The storks, disturbed by the noise, familiar though it be, take wing, wheel slowly about, beating for a moment, in silhouette on the yellow of the sky, their feathered fans; then return and perch on the points of the minarets, in their nests.

"Allah Akbar!" The cry, repeated for a long time, ceases at last, dies away in the engulfing silence ; the light quickly fades, yielding before a dusky blue which seems to rise from the ground; and from the side opposite to the town, from the side of darkness, from behind a thicket of cactus, comes the muted voice of a jackal in reply.

. . . .

In the time of Ramadan it is the custom in

Morocco to fill the night with music and feasting, after the austere fast of the day. Accordingly, as soon as the darkness has finally enveloped us, the town sends us the confused sounds of tabours beating strange dances, of bagpipes shrilling mournful songs. And in our little camp too, where the Ramadan is faithfully observed, issue from the tents the music of a two-stringed guitar, like the sound of a cricket in agony, and songs sung in piping voices, interspersed with clappings of hands.

A little later in the night the silence, which had returned, is suddenly filled with a harsh and heart-rending music, which seems to be in the air, to come from on high, to hover. Leaving my tent, I inquire of one of our muleteers, who is lingering in the starlight despite the lateness of the hour, whence these sounds proceed. Smiling, he points with his finger to the towers of the mosques which are outlined in grey on a sky sprinkled with a white powder of stars. At the top of each minaret, in company with the storks, a piper, it appears, is installed, piping with all his might, and due to continue till morning, above the confused darkness of the old town.

x

CHAPTER XXXVII

3rd May.

To-morrow we shall see Tangier the White again, the foreland of Europe, and the things and the people of this century.

This penultimate day's journey is long and arduous, under a sun much more oppressive than heretofore. Our old kaid, whom the fasts of Ramadan have well-nigh overcome, hesitates, is no longer sure of the way. Our muleteers, who are also abstaining from food, are unwontedly slow and somnolent. The distances grow between us, our little column lengthens in disquieting fashion, until it is strung out over a mile or two of hot and deserted country. Often we lose sight of the mules, the sleeping muleteers who follow us with our baggage and our presents from the Caliph, the famous presents which we prize so highly. Then, ourselves a little influenced by Ramadan, lacking courage to turn back in the heat, we lie down and wait for them, no matter where, but necessarily in the sun since there is no shade anywhere; no matter where on the old Arab earth, dry and burning, hiding our

322

heads in our white hoods, in the manner of shepherds taking a nap.

About three o'clock we are completely lost amid solitudes of bracken, mastics and lavender. There is now no sign of our tents or baggage, which must have followed another track. And our old kaid, whom we might have blamed for our mischance, fills us with pity in his stupor of fatigue.

. . . .

But, evening come and our way found again, the last of our encampments is such as to increase our regret at the termination of our wanderings in this primitive land of flowers and herbage.

In a place without a name, on the slope of a high hill, before a peaceful horizon, it is a kind of little circular plateau, a little terrace, which is surrounded by a hedge of palmetto as a garden by its fence. And on this plateau, Allah, for us, has spread a carpet of white and blue and rose, absolutely virgin, where the foot of man has never trod: Easter daisies, mallows, gentians, growing in such close-set masses that they produce the effect of marblings of flowers. The stalks are short and slender, on a sandy soil, tempting and soft to lie upon. The air is filled with sweet and healthy scents. There is, exceptionally, a wood crowning the hill that overlooks us, a wood of olives. Over the blue sky, which is beginning to pale, to turn to a limpid green, a tissue of little dappled clouds has been discreetly thrown like a veil. There is no sign of humanity anywhere; and the spot is the most fragrant, the most peaceful, that we have yet found in our journey. And it is for us alone, all this profusion of flowers, all this music of insects, all this resplendence of colours and of the air. This evening of May on this wild plateau has a peace of Eden; it is such an evening as must have been known in prehistoric springs, ere men had yet disfigured the earth.

CHAPTER XXXVIII

4th May.

AFTER another long day's march, under a burning sun, we see, towards evening, Tangier the White appearing in the distance; above it, the blue line of the Mediterranean, and above again, that far-off irisate denticulation which is the coast of Europe.

We experience a first impression of constraint, almost of surprise, in passing between the European villas of the outskirts. And our constraint becomes confusion when, on entering the garden of the hotel, with our travel-stained faces, our burnouses and bare legs, our following of muleteers and bales, our paraphernalia of nomad Bedouins, we find ourselves in the midst of a swarm of young English misses on the way to play lawn tennis.

And, truly, Tangier seems to us the height of civilisation, of modern refinement. A hotel, where we are given to eat without being required to produce the letter of ransom signed by the Sultan; where the couscous is brought to us, *à table d'hôte*, by dainty gentlemen in black clothes and white ties, with exiguous little caftans, cut short in front at the waist, as if the cost of cloth had been a consideration, and prolonged behind below the back in two absurd little pendants like the elytra of a cockchafer. And ugly things and convenient things. The town everywhere open and safe ; no longer need of guards in passing through the streets ; no longer need of personal watchfulness ; in short, a material existence very much simplified, more comfortable, we are forced to admit, easy to all with a little money. And in the pause that now is given us, we realise how oppressing, despite its charm, was this deep plunge we have just made into anterior ages.

Nevertheless, our preferences and our regrets are still for the country that has just closed behind us. For ourselves, it is too late, assuredly : we could never become acclimatised there. But the life of those who are born there seems to us less miserable than ours, and less false. Personally, I avow that I would rather be the most holy Caliph than president of the most parliamentary, the most cultured, the most industrious of republics. And even the least of the camel-drivers, who, after his courses through the desert, dies one fine day in the sun, stretching out trusting hands to Allah, seems to me to have played a far fairer part than a worker in the great European factory, be he

stoker or diplomat, who ends his martyrdom
of toil and greed blaspheming on a bed.

.   .   .   .

Oh, sombre Moghreb, do thou remain, for
many a long year yet, immured, impenetrable
to things that are new; turn thy back on
Europe and immobilise thyself in things of the
past.   Sleep on, sleep on, and continue thy old
dream, so that there may be at least one last
country where men lift up their hearts in
prayer.

And may Allah preserve to the Sultan his
unconquered territories, and his solitudes carpeted with flowers, his deserts of daffodils and
irises, that he may exercise there the agility
of his cavaliers and the muscles of his horses;
that he may wage war there as once the paladins,
and reap there his harvest of rebel heads.   May
Allah preserve to the Arab people its mystical
dreams, its disdainful immobility and its grey
rags.   May he preserve to the Bedouin bagpipes their mournful, harrowing sound; to the
old mosques their inviolable mystery—and
the shroud of white chalk to the ruins. . . .

Index

Index 329

*For Product Safety Concerns and Information please contact
our EU representative GPSR@taylorandfrancis.com Taylor & Francis
Verlag GmbH, Kaufingerstraße 24, 80331 München, Germany*

T - #0013 - 270225 - C0 - 234/156/18 [20] - CB - 9780710308160 - Gloss Lamination